Peasants in Transition: The Changing Economy of the Peruvian Aymara: A General Systems Approach

Ted Lewellen

The peasant transition from a subsistence-agriculture economy to a money economy is one of the most significant and widespread phenomena of the twentieth century. For the world's largest occupational group--comprising from one-half to two-thirds of the world's population--this process constitutes a fundamental transformation in terms of economic and social complexity.

The Aymara Indians of the Lake Titicaca Basin in Peru are presently undergoing such a transformation. Drawing upon thirteen months' fieldwork and on the most detailed economic data ever gathered for this area, Professor Lewellen shows why and how the Aymara have entered the money economy and the effects of this rapid change on social structure, religion, kinship, and world view. Several principles that might apply to a general model of peasant transition are suggested on the basis of comparison of the Aymara with peasant groups in other parts of the world.

The book is an important demonstration of the viability of General Systems Theory for anthropology. Among the surprising findings directly deriving from this approach is that the Aymara transition is a response not to inputs from the industrial sector, but to instabilities within the traditional Aymara economic system itself. The Systems Theory principle of the adaptive value of deviance is the basis for an in-depth analysis of the emergence of the Seventh-Day Adventists as a power-elite in many Aymara communities.

Ted Lewellen, assistant visiting professor of anthropology at Texas Tech University, received his Ph.D. in anthropology from the University of Colorado, Boulder.

Peasants in Transition

The Changing Economy of the Peruvian Aymara:
A General Systems Approach

Ted Lewellen

Westview Press
Boulder, Colorado

A Westview Replica Edition

Published in 1978 in the United States of America by

    Westview Press, Inc.
    5500 Central Avenue
    Boulder, Colorado 80301
    Frederick A. Praeger, Publisher and Editorial Director

Library of Congress Number: 78-343
ISBN: 0-89158-076-X

Printed and bound in the United States of America

Contents

viii

Tables and Figures

Acknowledgements

This research was partially funded by the
Instituto de Estudios Aymaras, under the direction
of Father Frank McGourn, a Maryknoll missionary.
The Institute arranged and paid for my language
training in Cochabamba, helped with field expenses,
and aided with introductions. Staff writer Victor
Ochoa and his wife, Brindice, were especially
helpful, as were the many bulletins they have written on Aymara culture. The Institute library in
Chucuito, which I used extensively, is probably one
of the best anywhere on the Aymara.

I got to know virtually all the Catholic missionaries then working in the Peruvian altiplano.
They housed me, fed me, entertained me, allowed
me to accompany them on their rounds in the campo,
and proved a valuable source of information on many
aspects of Aymara society. Above all, these
dedicated men and women provided the friendship that
made some long and frustrating months bearable.

My greatest thanks must be reserved for the
campesinos of the altiplano who allowed this absurd
gringo to live in their homes and communities for
months on end, to observe their meetings and church
services, and to ask them all sorts of ridiculous
questions. These people--one of the most maligned
in all anthropological literature (e.g., Trotter
1973, LaBarre 1966: 133)--exhibited their share of
kindness and humor to soften the inevitable
frustrations of field work. More, they showed me
that behind the veneer of alien customs and beliefs,
there is a basic humanity that I would be hard
pressed to define, but which will remain the
enduring discovery of my research.

Introduction

    The peasant transition from a subsistence agri-
culture economy to a money economy is one of the
most widespread phenomena of the twentieth century.
For the world's largest single occupational group,
comprising the vast majority of the peoples of the
developing countries, this process constitutes a
fundamental evolution in terms of economic and
social complexity.

    Such an evolution touches every aspect of
society. People who a short time ago were economically self-sufficient have become a major source of
wage labor for industrializing nations. Everywhere, once docile--or alternately dormant and
violently erupting--peasants are making their voices
heard in national political processes. Country-
sides, where only the baying of a mule or the ripple
of wind on rows of barley could be heard after dark,
now resound with the latest song hits or play-by-
play soccer games from radios purchased in big
city markets. Men who dared not dream beyond a
new horse or a good stud bull now pray for a motorcycle or even a truck. Farmers aid their ancient
rituals to the Earth Mother with chemical fertilizers, and native <u>curanderos</u> routinely prescribe

penicillin along with their herbs and rites. Extended families dissolve and new cohesions and loyalties form along non-kin lines. Indigenous religions either lose their authority or assume a host of new functions.

Despite the massiveness of this process, if only in terms of sheer numbers of people involved-- an estimated one-half to two-thirds of the world's population (Gamst 1974: 1)--and despite the importance to Third World government policy of understanding the dynamics of this transition, little exists in the way of an anthropological model or general theory.

To be sure, the economists have developed mathematical and graphic models to predict change along several alternative lines of development (e.g., Fisk and Shand 1965). The anthropologist might jealously admire the elegant simplicity of such models, but his world--that which his discipline has defined, or failed to define, for him--is not simple. He can not, for example, deal with even the most abstracted Economic Man, but must admit a man who is liable to maximize not merely economic benefits but status, security, or something virtually unfathomable. The economist might well demonstrate graphically that if you admit such and such economic inputs into the system then you can expect such and such outputs. The anthropologist, however, is stuck with such difficult-to-measure variables as kinship, religion, world view, tradition, temperment, sodalities, and inheritance patterns.

But perhaps it is too early for general models. Peasants, like other peoples, have an irritating

2

tendency to wriggle out of any categories into which
they are too hastily confined. Already the definitions of Kroeber, Redfield, and even George Foster
have become "classical"--i.e., respectfully, vener-
ably outmoded. Characterizations of peasants in
terms of a "folk-urban continuum" or "great and
little traditions" or an "image of limited good"
seem, perhaps as true as ever, but somehow too simple,
somehow missing the point. Today the emphasis is,
as it must be, on change and complexity, and change
is difficult to get hold of. As soon as we general-
ize that peasants enter the modern economy because
of external stimuli, someone says, "Wait a minute;
in this community it was pressures from within the
system that forced the transition." As soon as
we develop a model in which regional markets are
the primary means of entry into the money economy,
someone protests, "But in this case it was the sale
of labor in distant industrial markets that was the
medium of transformation." Anthropologists may
discover an inner logic to kinship patterns or
myth, but change, by its very nature, will not stop
long enough to casually reveal its eternal essense.

Nor does this study attempt a grandiose model;
it is for the most part a description and analysis
of the socio-economic transition of the Aymara
Indians of the Lake Titicaca Basin in Peru. However, a wealth of ethnographic studies of peasants
in all parts of the world is available, and these
comparative data suggest that generalizations may
indeed be possible--for example, in regards to the
role of short-term migration to industrial centers.
On the other hand, so much material inevitably
evokes contradictions and controversies, partly

3

arising out of specific conditions peculiar to
particular peoples, but also emerging from contrary
interpretations. There are strongly differing
opinions on the extent to which the stimulus for
economic transformation lies within the peasant
system itself or in the wider environment, on the
degree to which short-term migration leads to disruption of the family, and whether or not such
migration is a transitional phase to the complete
"proletarianization" of the peasant.

In the concluding chapter I will attempt to
confront these problems and suggest some generalizations that may have cross-cultural validity.
This is not merely an academic exercise. A coherent
theory of the peasant transition would be a valuable
aid to Third World governments attempting to develop
a realistic policy toward their peasant majorities.
It is toward such a theory that this book is,
hesitantly but optimistically, dedicated.

The theoretical basis for this study is general
systems theory. Unlike functionalism or structural-
ism, which learned rather late to treat of diachronic
situations, systems theory is designed to deal with
change--even to the extent of postulating the
absolute necessity for change if any system is to
survive.* Also, unlike anthropological theories,
such as evolutionism, which deal with vast changes

---

*This is based on the concept of "entropy"--that
every closed system will tend toward its most statistically probable state, i.e., chaos. In order to
retain its state of organization and differentiation, an open system is continually "sucking
orderliness from its environment" (Rapaport 1968:
146).

4

over long periods of time, systems theory is applicable to small groups and, as we shall see, is amenable to extensive quantification.

Actually "systems theory" is a misnomer, if "theory" is taken to mean a set of explanatory principles, such as the "theory of evolution" or Steward's "theory of culture change". In comparison, systems theory is empty, void of content, not so much a hypothetical explanation as a framework, a set of organizing principles by which to better comprehend raw data. Much of systems theory has sifted into anthropology so subtly that it now seems mere common sense. It is difficult to recall that only a few decades ago, unilineal causality between two elements was the dominant form of scientific explanation, and feedback was unheard of; or to remember the days when "inputs" and "outputs" were computer jargon.

I have not restricted myself to that part of systems theory that has entered the mainstream of anthropology, but have taken this orientation as a new paradigm. For example, the following systems concepts are crucial to my argument: the hierarchy of systems, boundaries (or "essential variables") and the relative plasticity of these boundaries, "filters" (in the sense that inputs and outputs are blocked or distorted), closed and open systems, morphostasis and morphogenesis, and--central to my analysis of the Protestant elite --the adaptive value of a "pool of variability."

Though there is nothing particularly complex about any of these concepts, which will be defined as they are used, together they form a powerful set of tools for examining society in change. But

can they really tell us something we could not have
discovered by more conventional analysis? An example
is in order. William Carter (1965b) discovered and
documented almost the same type of Protestant elite
in Bolivia that I found on the island of Soqa in
Peru. However, according to conventional theory and
to the prevailing belief that Protestants must be
marginals in Catholic-dominated countries, these
people had to be suffering from anomie and dis-
illusionment, they had to be on their way out.
Actually, precisely the opposite is the case, but
to understand why requires a theoretical orientation
not available when Carter studied, one that views
deviance as adaptive, not necessarily dysfunctional.
Another example: the changes which are the subject
of this book are massive, involving the entire
socio-economic system, and have been in process for
twenty years or more. Yet, despite the high quality
of recent anthropology done in the Peruvian
altiplano, this transformation has not, to my
knowledge, been described or even identified. We
are all trapped within the limits of our paradigms.
I suspect that, in this case, a systems orientation
made visible what was not evident via more static
paradigms.

    This is not to suggest that systems theory is
a panacea, or that it can replace long-established
theories and methods. To the contrary, I found
that classic functional and structural explanations
were sometimes in order, and that old-fashioned
hypothesis-testing remains invaluable. If systems
theory is not to become simply a new set of
blinders, it must make no claim to exclusivity.
It can extend our vision, but it should not

obscure other points of view.

I first visited the Peruvian altiplano in the summer of 1974, when the Instituto de Estudios Aymaras (IDEA), a Catholic research organization, brought me down to teach classes in anthropology to the missionaries. I was able to visit most of the mission houses around Lake Titicaca, and, through the guidance of the missionaries, to visit the campo (countryside) and meet some of the people. A year later I returned, again under the auspices of IDEA, and conducted research between July 15, 1975, and November 15, 1976, including five months in language school in Cochabamba, Bolivia, studying Spanish and, briefly, Aymara.

Between sessions of language school, I made a two-month preliminary survey of the Lake Titicaca area, and at that time decided on my problem and my area of research. When I returned again from Cochabamba, using contacts made on the previous visit, I was able to establish myself with a family in the island community of Soqa. After four months, I moved into the small town of Acora where I could coordinate the giving of a questionnaire in three communities. Later, I conducted follow-up interviews in all three communities. In addition, I was able to have a land-and-cattle questionnaire given in Soqa by local sector leaders. Because of the way the data was gathered--that is, by trusted leaders in the respective communities--I believe this is the most accurate economic data ever to come out of the Aymara campo. Details on how these data were collected and analyzed will be found in Appendix A.

Like most other anthropologists who have
worked in this area, I at first believed Aymara
society to be relatively static. The biculturalism
so well described by Hickman (1963, 1971) was
obvious, but there was little evidence of any massive or fundamental change in the system itself.
Thus, my questionnaire was written largely to test
certain Weberian economic hypotheses in relation
to Protestantism and Catholicism. It was only
after I began to collect, quantify, and analyze
the data from the questionnaire and follow-up
interviews that it became evident that I had--
inadvertantly--happened on to a fundamental evolution
in Aymara economy and social structure. From this
point, the research took a different shape.
The socio-economic transformation assumed central
place, while the original problem--the Catholic-
Protestant comparison--came to be viewed as one
example of this all-pervading process. While the
emergence of an Adventist elite in a place where,
according to conventional theory, Protestants are
supposed to be persecuted marginals, may be interesting of itself, it can only be understood in
relation to economic and social changes that seem
quite removed from the religious sphere.

Here, then, is an analysis of one society
undergoing a transition that is taking place in
every part of the world. If universals are indeed
contained in particulars, it is hoped that the
Aymara case may suggest some dynamics applicable in
other parts of Latin America, in Africa, in Asia....

8

1. The Physical and Historical Setting

A tourist passing through Acora would hardly
notice it. It is but one of several such towns,
mere groupings of mud-walled houses and shops, that
dot the unpaved section of the Pan American Highway
between Puno and Juli in southern Peru. In the dry
winter months, roughly from May through September,
the town is gray with dust from the wheels of the
passenger-and-cargo bearing trucks that pass through
at all hours, the leaden monochrome broken only by
the colorful skirts and shawls of the women who
sell oranges or grapes or apples at the corners of
the barren plaza. Saturday the town is enlivened
by a cattle market on the pampa, the flat plain,
a quarter mile to the north. On Sunday, market day,
the plaza is mobbed with sellers and buyers of beans,
bicycle parts, school books, plastic shoes and
rubber-tire sandals, tools, needles and thread,
cheap machine-made cotton shirts and pants, almost
anything a campesino might need. But weekdays,
except for a few drinkers at the tiny shops that
line the square selling sweetened alcohol by the
glass, the town is silent and deserted.

In ancient times, before Inca domination,
Acora was a commercial center, founded, according to

tradition, by Cari, chief of the Lupaca tribe.
Today it is what the Spanish call a poblacho--a
dirty, insignificant little town.

Acora is the jumping-off place and center of
minimal commerce for the community of Soqa, fifteen
miles to the east by a road passable for vehicles.
Campesinos, who must travel on foot or bicycle,
prefer the shorter ten-mile road. In the wet
season, when even bicycles are an impossibility,
this distance requires a four- or five-hour walk--
stops for bread and conversation included--
trudging up to one's ankles in mud and removing
one's pants to ford waist-deep streams. From late
June on, it is but two hours by bicycle.

The gutted road runs straight out onto the
pampa, and once away from the town one can
easily understand why this area is called the
altiplano, the high plain. High it is, almost
exactly 12,500 feet above sea level. Yet the
country here resembles more the hilly deserts of
New Mexico than, say, the Rocky Mountains. From
the Acora pampa the high mountain chains, the
cordilleras, are not even visible. There is only
the plain, bristled with brown ichu grass, stretching away on every side to dry hills, their bases
glimmering with the scattered corrugated metal
roofs of small communities.

The road runs through two deep and, in winter,
almost dry stream beds, past a lake where there is
always a flock of flamingos, like a pink island in
a pointilist painting, past a primary school, and
climbs abruptly so that it is necessary to dismount
and walk one's bicycle. At the top of the hill,
an arm of Lake Titicaca appears, but the larger

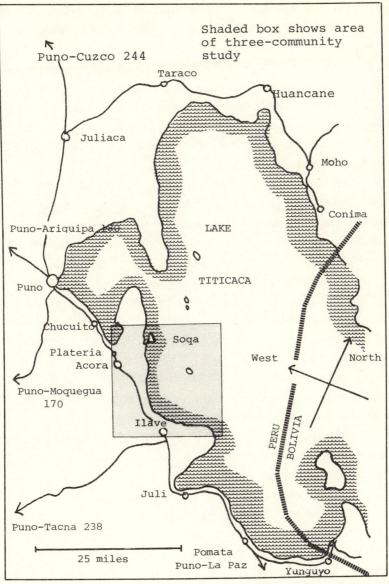

Figure 1.1   Lake Titicaca Basin

From Hickman 1963: xvi

11

part of the lake, in front and to the south, remains
hidden behind a high, jagged wall of tortured rock
about three kilometers ahead. The road leads down
again, past thatch-roofed complexes of houses, past
grazing cattle and sheep, past women in red or green
skirts and multi-colored shawls; it crosses a valley
and rises abruptly up the rugged hill, the path so
rocky here that a bicycle must be shouldered and
carried most of the way.

Topping the crest, an amazing scene suddenly
opens up. The lake appears, the twentieth largest
fresh-water lake in the world, a hundred forty
miles long, thirty-five miles across, its vast,
incredibly blue expanse broken to the north by the
Capachica Peninsula and the islands of Amantani
and Taquili.

Below, and slightly to the south, the island
of Soqa juts into the lake like a huge, roughly-
hewn hammer, its "head" a line of high, sheer
cliffs, silhouetted by the distant white profile
of 21,000-foot Mount Iliampu, in Bolivia on the
other side of the lake. From here the island seems
a peninsula, but it is a true island, connected to
the mainland by a hundred-yard causeway, dry now,
but in summer knee-deep under icy lake water.

The houses on the island, about 270 of them
--from here but tiny squares--are not centralized
but are scattered evenly about the arable part of
the land, this side of the cliffs. People and
cattle, mere dots in the distance, move among the
dry fields. Except for some metal roofs, the view
might be exactly the same as that seen by an Inca
traveler four-and-a-half centuries ago. The island
community seems to exist in some perpetual pastoral

12

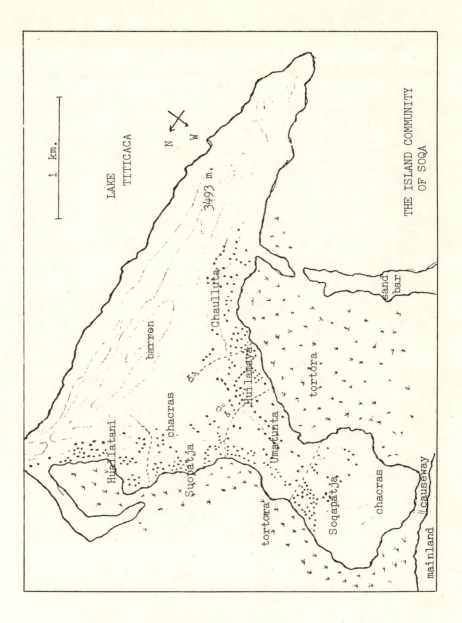

Figure 1.2   Soqa

serenity, outside of time, as though nothing has
fundamentally changed in millenia.

The image is illusory. Everything is changing.

The socio-economic system of the Peruvian
Aymara is presently undergoing a rapid and fundamental transformation. After four hundred years of
isolation--enforced from without by persecution,
exploitation, and bigotry, and from within by
suspicion, hostility, and fear--the Aymara are
moving from their closed agricultural communities
into the wider world of the money economy, a world
characterized by circular migration to the coast,
increased contact with once remote mestizos,
entirely new local government structures, and such
peculiar religious changes as the development of
a minority Protestant elite.

That change should arrive so late is not
surprising, given the geographical and cultural
barriers which have long cut off the Aymara from
the mainstream of Peruvian history. The Andes in
the region of Lake Titicaca, on the border of
Peru and Bolivia, hardly resemble North American
conceptions of "mountains." Rather, they are like
an enormous lump, over four hundred kilometers
across, rising dry and virtually vegetationless
from the Pacific deserts to a relatively level
plain, then dropping precipitately on the eastern
side, in a series of jagged peaks and lush valleys,
to the vast jungle below. On top of this "lump,"
extending along either side, are two mountain
chains, the Maritime Cordillera to the west and,
to the east, the awesome Cordillera Real. Between
these two towering white walls lies the altiplano,

14

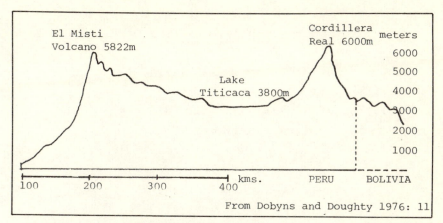

Figure 1.3   Profile of the Andes in the region of
              Lake Titicaca

stretching hundreds of miles south of Cuzco
into Bolivia, a dry, barren region of pampas, hills,
and plateaus, at an altitude of 12,500 feet (the
level of the lake) and up.

   Little grows naturally here: the pampas are
covered by clumps of tola and yareta bushes and
course ichu grass, poor forage for any but
indigenous llamas and alpacas. There are essentially
two seasons, rainy and dry, roughly winter and
summer. Hickman (1971: 5) calculated a 45° F.
annual mean temperature, with a range of 40° to
65° for twenty-four hours for the planting months
of October to April, and 35° to 65° for the May
to September dry months. It can get colder; I
have seen snow, several inches deep, stay on the
ground for days in late August and early September.

   The population of this area, specifically in
the department of Puno, reflects patterns long
outmoded for Peru considered as a whole. Whereas
the nation is now almost 60% urban--a statistic
reflecting the internal colonialism of Lima, which

15

drains both human and physical resources from the
rest of the country--Puno remains a mere 24% urban,
and many of these "urban" residents live in tiny
pueblos. For the district of Acora, in which lie
two of the communities of this study, out of a
population of 28,963 only 1,510 are "urban;" the
other 95% are rural peasants, living in numerous
small communities, mostly mere collections of
houses with perhaps a school but lacking a plaza
or even a store (ONEC 1972: 2, 46, 60).

The department of Puno's total population of
779,564 (ibid: 2) is large, considering that the
vast majority of these people are crowded about the
shores of the lake, where agriculture is so intensive
that most fields are never allowed to go fallow,
and in many areas there is such a scarcity of
grazing land that cattle are tied in the potato
fields and fed lakeweed and tortora. A tall reed
that grows profusely in the lake, tortora furnishes
not only cattle food, but is eaten by campesinos
during the hard months before harvest and used to
thatch roofs and to construct balsas, canoe-shaped
reed boats, so familiar from travel posters of
Lake Titicaca.

There is a rigid class division between Indian
campesinos and mixed-blood mestizos, the latter
comprising the large landholding, entrepreneurial,
industrial, and urban class which has, for
centuries, been in a position to dominate and
oppress the peasant class. Intermediary between
these two groups are the cholos, a term with
derogatory connotations, but the only term available.
These are people who have repudiated their
campesino origins and have assumed mestizo dress,

16

language, and values. Despite their reputation for being "campesinos on the make," cholos form a class of often ambitious entrepreneurs--store owners, small factory owners, truck drivers, and contrabandistas--that is extensively involved in the economy of the altiplano.

The peasants, in contrast, have not been so involved, at least until very recently. Growing for their own families' subsistence, with no specialization for market sales, Aymara peasants have only minimally participated in the national economy. Their closed, unvarying life, tied to the yearly agricultural cycle, was the Aymara pattern of culture for many hundreds of years.

Present-day Aymara are the direct descendants of a number of tribes that inhabited the lake region since pre-Inca times. The largest of these were the Colla and Lupaca, who were deadly rivals. When Viracocha began expansion of the Inca empire about 1430, chiefs of both these tribes recognized the power of this new military force from the north, and tried to ally themselves with it. Viracocha chose alliance with the Colla, stimulating an attack by the Lupaca which killed the Colla chief. When Viracocha arrived to render punishment, the Lupaca quickly made a pact with the Incas. Thus the larger part of the early conquest of the Titicaca Basin was accomplished without warfare on the part of the conquering empire.

Chucuito, the Lupaca capital, thus became the capital of Collasuyu, the southeastern and largest of the four quarters into which the Inca empire or Tahuantinsuyu (literally, "Land of the Four

Quarters") was divided, an area extending from the Titicaca Basin over most of Bolivia and into northwest Argentina and northern Chile.

Even under the yoke of the Inca, the Aymara commenced the pattern of violent rebellion that characterizes them to the present day. Though supposedly already "conquered" by peaceful means, the Colla and Lupaca had to be forcibly reconquered twice. Later, during the reign of Huayna Capac (1493-1527), Aymara troops were trusted enough to be permitted to fight in the Inca armies under their own leaders. In the Inca civil war, the Aymara sided with Huascar against the briefly victorious Atahualpa.

In the early stages of the Spanish conquest, the Titicaca region was reconnoitered by an important military expedition under Diego de Almagro, but the Spaniards went on to explore south, later to return to attack Cuzco and embroil themselves in a series of civil wars, leaving the Aymara to their own devices. With the defeat of Manco Inca--the puppet ruler who took charge of the Inca forces and turned them against his Spanish masters--the Lupaca asserted their independence by attacking their age-old enemies, the Colla. The latter requested Spanish aid, thus paving the way for easy Spanish domination of the area.

For centuries during which civilizations rose and fell and conquest followed conquest, peasant culture remained relatively unchanged. The basic Andean social unit, the ayllu--a group of kin that held land in common--persisted intact. Such continuity was hardly contested, except by disease, during the years that immediately followed the

18

defeat of Tahuantinsuyu. The Spanish abolished the Inca religion without replacing it with Christianity, so many Indians simply reverted to pre-Inca religious patterns. The energies of the conquerors were expended in internecine wars, gold hunting, and establishing cities, so they maintained authority in remote rural areas only through local Indian leaders, thus permitting a lesser cultural unification of Andean populations than had been the case under direct rule by the Incas.

This situation lasted only until 1572, when Viceroy Francisco de Toledo defeated the last remnants of Inca opposition, finally permitting a transition from "conquest culture" to true colonial culture. Since the economic system that financed the viceroyalty was based on Indian labor and tribute, the history of this era is one of brutal, but routine, exploitation and oppression.

Toledo was the fifth Spanish viceroy of Peru, but the first strong leader, and the first to try seriously to centralize authority. In their rural isolation, Indians were vulnerable to all sorts of depredations by the ravenous Spanish. Supposedly to protect them, as well as make their religious conversion easier, Toledo had the Indians gathered in urban centers called reducciones, where they were overseen by administrative officials called corregidores. This move made it easier for the Spanish to seize deserted lands. Whatever good intentions might be claimed for the reduccion program, little in that direction can be claimed for Toledo's version of the Inca mita, Spanish Colonialism's "most deadly dimension, after Old World diseases, for the Peruvian Indians" (Dobyns and Doughty 1976:

100). According to legal statutes, the corregidor
was to impress one seventh of the adult male Indians
of his region into the mita system of forced labor.
For the altiplano, mita came to signify mita de
minas, forced labor in the silver mines at Potosí
or Carabaya and, later, at the mercury mine at
Huancavelica. LaBarre (1948: 31) estimates that
over 14% of the Aymara were in forced labor in the
mines at any one time. The mita de minas was
virtually a capital sentence: there was a death rate
of two out of three mitayos at Potosí where workers
were forced to live chained together in the shaft
for five days, without seeing daylight. Work was
supposedly for a year, but one could seldom accom-
plish production quotas in a year, even with wife
and children helping. Yet it was not Potosí, but
Huancavelica that was called the "mine of death;"
the high grade mercury ore was so poisonous that
even families living near the mine suffered the
effects. It has been estimated that the Indian
population of Chucuito shrank by two-thirds between
1628 and 1754 because of the mitas (Dew 1969: 21).

The Church offered little opposition to such
horrors. Contrary to present belief, most priests
were not missionaries and had little to do with
uprooting idolatry or converting natives. Rather,
most of them served Spanish populations, living in
cities or attaching themselves to wealthy encomenderos. There were, however, a few, mainly Jesuits,
who actively protested against the exploitation,
a transgression which--along with becoming too
wealthy and influential themselves--got them expelled from all America in 1767. This left the
Indians of the altiplano with no protectors. Added

to the mita, to virtual slavery on vast encomiendas,
and to burdensome taxation, came the repartamiento,
the forced sale of goods to Indians at inflated
prices. The eighteenth century had turned out worse,
if possible, than the century of conquest.

Around 1776 there were a series of violent
protests, most of them easily crushed. A few were
substantial. In 1780 the Aymara joined the Quechua
in a brutal millenarian movement led by an Inca
descendant who called himself Tupac Amaru II. Whole
regions of the altiplano were depopulated. Chucuito
was burned to the ground. And even after the kill-
ing was done--that is, after Tupac Amaru and his
family were publicly tortured to death by the
victorious Spaniards--epidemic after epidemic swept
the war-ravaged area, further decimating it. Three
years later, Tupac Amaru's nephew led a revolt in
Azangaro, burned Huancane' to the ground and be-
sieged Puno. In 1814, Mateo Garcia Pumacahua cap-
tured Puno and marched on La Paz. These rebellions,
and the diseases that followed in their wake, deci-
mated the Aymara without substantially changing the
oppression under which they lived. Ethnic prejudices and hatreds remained so strong that Indian
rebellions with general aims collapsed into
slaughters of all whites and mestizos, frightening
off the support and possible leadership that might
have led to success.

Meanwhile, the whites and mestizos were having
their own rebellion. The war of independence had
little significance for the Indians, except that
they were required to fight on whichever side demanded their help. It was largely a power struggle
between the creoles (American-born Spaniards) and

21

the chapatones (Spain-born administrators). However,
certain reforms did affect the Indians. In 1821,
San Martin, somewhat prematurely, declared Peru to
be independent, and at the same time abolished all
personal service required of the Indians, including
household tasks for encomenderos and, far more
important, the dreaded mita de minas. He also out-
lawed the term "Indian" and declared all campesinos
to be equal Peruvian citizens, a purely rhetorical
equality, as it turned out. None of San Martin's
reforms, which were largely ignored, had anything
near the impact on the altiplano as one mandate of
Simon Bolivar: after the battle of Ayacucho in 1824,
from which Peru dates its independence, Bolivar
declared Indians to be individual owners of the
ayllu lands they occupied. This declaration had
the effect of breaking up the ayllu holdings and
creating competition between Indians and mestizos
for land, a competition the mestizos usually won
if they were willing to pay the price of a judge and
a few professional witnesses. At the same time, the
introduction of Spanish inheritance patterns, in
which sons and daughters inherit equally, set
in motion an increasing fragmentation of land.
Bolivar's directive was reasserted by the Constitutional Congress of 1825.

The battle of Ayacucho did not end warfare in
the altiplano. After 1825, the department of Puno,
following the successful example of Bolivia, em-
barked on a series of attempts to secede from Peru,
ravaging the altiplano with near constant warfare
until the last of these rebellions was put down in
1842. Nor was that the end of strife. The age of
caudillismo--of political bosses and private

22

armies--was ushered in with independence from Spain,
so that for scores of years Peru continued to be
devastated by innumerable civil wars.

Except for its periodic use as a battleground,
the altiplano remained effectively isolated from
Peruvian politics and economy until the great "guano
boom" that lasted from 1840 to 1879. The discovery
that the immense concentrations of bird dung on
Peruvian-owned islands were exceedingly potent
fertilizer brought the incipient nation a sudden
wealth to approach its golden past. During this
period a number of public works projects were fi-
financed, including the Matarani-Ariquipa-Juliaca-
Puno railroad which, for the first time, offered
relatively easy transportation to and from the
coast.

Meanwhile, on the political front, wealth
stimulated some long overdue--and generally mis-
guided--Indian legislation. Following San Martin's
example, the 1852 Civil Code gave Indians full
citizenship, but in bestowing upon them the rights
of other citizens, it also took away some of the
essential protections that they had enjoyed as a
special people, leaving them more than ever open
to exploitation. Two years later, President Ramon
Castilla ended the collection of Indian tribute
which had been used to support local government,
which added to the power of the central bureaucracy
in Lima. It was only after 1895 that this "internal
colonialism"--the concentration of wealth and man-
power in one city--began to take the form of massive migrations from sierra to coast. Population
pressure on the land was beginning to be felt, and
opportunities in cities, never before available on

23

a large scale, appeared with the inception of industry.

The many constant changes in Indian legislation in the twentieth century have been confusing, not least for the people to whom they are aimed, but several items have been significant, nevertheless. Augusto Leguía, on assuming the office of president in 1919, set up a Bureau of Indian Affairs, and in 1920 the government, to protect the Indians from further encroachment on their land by hacienda owners, created the system of comunidades indigenas, a system reaffirmed by the Constitution of 1933 and the Civil Code of 1936 (though by 1960 there were still only thirty-nine such communities recognized by the government, and less than half of these were in the altiplano). Also under the Leguía government significant legislation was passed suppressing the personal services of Indians to local authorities, abolishing the faenas (required works), and suppressing the power of local authorities over the Indians. These measures notably diminished abuses of mestizos against peasants and precipitated a process of favorable change that has continued to this day.

Equally significant, Leguía initiated a large-scale road-building program, using forced peasant labor. It was during this time that most of the roads in the altiplano, and those connecting the altiplano with the coast, were built.

Such changes were hardly enough to placate the Indians, who continued to explode in violent revolt every so many years, like an alternately dormant and erupting volcano. Major revolts took place in the 1870's, in 1886, 1903, and 1928. The latter two,

24

which devastated the area around Lake Titicaca, including Plateria and Ilave, and extended north to Cuzco, were caused by more or less arbitrary exactions of taxes by the governor of the department of Puno and by unpaid prefects and subprefects who earned their incomes through such taxes. Even as late as 1945, outbreaks occurred in Azangaro and Chucuito.

As usual, these bloody affairs had little lasting effect, but the campesino was indeed becoming increasingly politicized. In the thirties and forties, policy debates and political conflicts of national importance between the socialist APRA party and more conservative groups offered hope to the natives, but ended in a debacle when APRA sold out to its former enemies for purely political reasons. However, the rhetoric of the Bolivian revolution of 1952--the only true economic and social revolution to survive on the continent-- reached the most remote campesino, across the lake by radio or by road via contraband traffic.

The Aymara were becoming politically sophisticated, at least relative to their previous state of total ignorance in such matters, and they soon proved it. In 1955 and 1956 the altiplano suffered a devastating drought, which not only led to extensive migration, but also politicized enough campesinos that they were able to send their own representatives to parliment to represent their interests.

Substantial change did not come until the coup by General Juan Velasco Alverado against President Fernando Belaunde Terry on October 3, 1968, when Latin America witnessed the anomalous spectacle of

25

a military dictatorship that was not only left-leaning but also truly revolutionary. Under Velasco, the government nationalized or made a forced purchase of the fishing industry, oil, railroads, communications, and electric companies, among other things. To further break the chains of foreign economic domination, Velasco sharply reduced imports and attempted to build up Peru's own industry, with the requirement that all industry be at least 51% controlled by Peruvian investors. In this way, a large auto assembly industry grew up, with what was to be built determined by the government. A state monopoly on mineral marketing was formed. It was required by law that all foreign currency accounts be converted into soles. At the same time, Velasco stopped well this side of communism (and perhaps this side of the type of massive U.S. economic intervention that helped overthrow Allende in Chile), encouraging a stock exchange, large-scale investment by the wealthy, and a populist small-scale capitalism.

For the umpteenth time, and with the usual effect, Velasco declared that in Peru there were no more Indios--a term that just will not seem to go away. His agricultural reforms were more significant: he expropriated the largest land holdings, and those haciendas that were most notoriously repressive, paying owners in bonds convertible to industrial investment or urban improvement, and cooperativizing the land among the peasants.

These reforms had little effect on the Titicaca Basin campesinos, almost all of whom are freeholding land owners. However, SINAMOS, the government's social action arm, has intensified efforts to

26

integrate more communities into the comunidad
indigena program, dating from 1920, and now called
comunidades reconocidos (recognized communities),
offering special work permits and loan privileges
for those communities that comply. SINAMOS has also
built numerous roads in the campo, constructed
markets, and promoted health and adult education.
However, the organization remains distrusted by
campesinos, not only as an historically conditioned
distrust of all government, but also as a reaction
against the arrogance of SINAMOS operatives, who are
usually hated mestizos, and against the incompetence
of the bureaucracy itself.

Velasco's budget was close to twice that of
his predecessor because of overspending, inter-
national inflation, and the problems of rapid, and
not always efficient, change. Peru plunged near
bankruptcy. Faced with economic problems beyond his
control, Velasco was deposed in 1975 by his prime
minister, General Francisco Morales Bermúdez.

Under Morales, Peru is leaning again to the
right, seeking buyers for many of the industries
previously nationalized. A long overdue devaluation
of the sol, from 43.8 to 65 to the dollar (with
the latter figure going higher by the week in
November 1976), increased the cost of living by
50%, and this continues to rise. Shortages are
commonplace because of the low production of Peruvian industry and some illegal strikes (e.g., of
the fishermen), but the government retains its
tight clamp on imports. The situation is sufficiently explosive that when this researcher left
Peru in mid-November 1976, there had been a suspen-
sion of constitutional guarantees, and Lima had

been under a curfew, for several months.

When a community in the altiplano becomes reconocido, SINAMOS erects a large stucco sign beside the road and paints it in bright colors with pictures of determined-looking campesinos breaking their chains or rushing off to battle with rifles in hand. Beside the picture there is always a brief slogan. On one of these signs, for a community off the Pan American Highway just north of Ilave, there is the slogan:

HACER REVOLUCIÓN ES DEFENDER LA PATRIA. This Orwellian phrase summarizes the situation today: "To make revolution is to defend the country."

2. A System in Transition

The physical boundaries of Soqa are easy enough
to describe: it is an island, bounded on all sides
by Lake Titicaca. Other Aymara communities, while
not so obviously delimited, still have their physical boundaries.

But these are not the most important boundaries for the Aymara community if we extend the
definition of "boundaries" to include all those
elements that delimit the system, in the sense of
blocking or filtering inputs from the outside world
and containing the interactions of those within the
community. Given this wider definition, boundaries
are no longer so concrete, and they are, to some
extent, arbitrary. To determine a group's
boundaries, we must first acknowledge a hierarchy of
systems, each of which is a sub-system of a larger
system, so that the level we choose to study will
not be some absolute entity, but one selected
according to the particular needs of the researcher.
Even then, there may be a vast number of physical,
social, economic, cultural, and linguistic boundaries so that the selection of a few will be dependent on the observer.

Nevertheless, if we are dealing with an

integrated system, a few boundaries will stand out
as quite obvious, and these are by no means entirely
arbitrary; we can state with some precision how
these elements wholly or partially obstruct interactions between the system and its environment.
These elements provide a minimal definition of the
system, to the extent that if they change radically,
the system must be redefined. For this reason, such
boundaries are sometimes termed essential variables
--"essential" in the sense of being fundamental
properties of the system.

If we examine the traditional Aymara system,
as it has existed since conquest times, the essential
variables might be described as follows:

1. Subsistence agriculture and animal husbandry.
The family lived almost entirely by its own produce.
Crops were grown with only the family's consumption
in mind. Though surpluses might be sold or bartered
in regional markets, there was no specialization of
crops for marketing. Animals were also raised only
for family consumption, that is, for food, wool,
and labor. Money played a minimal or irrelevant
role in this economy.

2. The ayllu form of government. These extended lineages were loosely defined but constantly reinforced by fiestas. The system was headed by a
hilacata who was at once ritual and administrative
leader. Though ayllu lands were originally held
communally and broken up and given to individuals
in the early Republican Period, the ayllu remained
a physically defined area, as the community is today.

3. A pagan-to-Catholic religious continuum. The
indigenous religion exists side-by-side with an
extremely popularized Catholicism, mostly manifested

30

in the fiesta system. There is some syncretism
but, since each religion serves different functions,
they are usually called into play at different times
and for different ends.

4. The Aymara language. Until nearly the
middle of this century, Aymara was spoken almost
exclusively by the Aymara people, making a verbal
communications barrier between them and mestizos
almost absolute. Even today, only a minority of
campo women speak more than a few words of Spanish.

5. A limited population. By this I mean that
there are population parameters beyond which the
system could not be sustained. While the population
of the altiplano has been growing exponentially for
more than a hundred years, the rate has been less
than for the rest of Peru.

6. A relatively closed system. This is not
so much a boundary as a property of the other
essential variables considered together. Nevertheless, the fact that the system has only allowed the
most minimal inputs from its wider social environment is crucial enough to be considered separately.
No social system is truly closed; all must respond
to inputs, so the relative degree of closure depends
on the extent to which these inputs are blocked or
filtered. By this definition, the Aymara community
was, relatively speaking, very closed.

All social systems are in the process of constant change. The type of change depends on the
degree to which the boundaries are affected. If, as
in most traditional societies, changes take place
largely or only within the boundaries, we may speak
of "morphostasis," a process by which change sustains
the status quo. Such systems will interact with

31

their environments largely through negative feedback (deviation minimizing) processes.

A second type of change, often, but not necessarily, characterized by positive feedback (deviation amplification), is that in which the boundaries themselves are "struck," so to speak. Boundaries must have some elasticity if they are not to fall apart at the first challenge, so a social system, even the most rigid, can sustain a certain degree of change in one or two essential variables without being particularly threatened. However, if many essential variables change radically--and since they are all interrelated we would expect a radical change in one to affect the others--then we get a process of "morphogenesis." This means that the system has been pushed beyond what Easton (1965: 24) refers to as the "critical range." The system will cease to exist or change sufficiently that it needs to be redefined.

The Aymara system is presently undergoing morphogenesis. The boundaries have been struck; they have been struck hard and suddenly. The changes that are taking place in the system are fundamental, that is, they are of the essential variables themselves. These changes will continue until the system accomplishes a new steady state, one that will be significantly different in economy, social structure, and ideology than that of traditional Aymara society.

Change in this case does not mean collapse, except perhaps of some specific variables, such as the subsistence agriculture subsystem. It certainly does not mean cultural collapse. Indeed, the Aymara seem to be adapting to these changes not merely smoothly but, in some cases, enthusiastically.

The evidence that this is happening is, I believe, overwhelming, but it is complicated by a dearth of accurate statistics from the past with which to compare the statistics I gathered. Those statistics that do exist are not precisely comparable to my own, but even rough comparisons can suggest what is happening and how fast it is happening.

According to one study, annual effective income for campesinos in southern Peru was $37* (Schaedel 1967: 26), a figure probably based on the 1961 census. Hickman (1971: 200), in his 1962 study, tried to elicit how much money entered the average household per year, but found people reluctant to answer because of fear taxes would be imposed and because money came in so irregularly no one had the slightest idea how much was earned over any given period of time. Hickman, with two years residence in the campo upon which to base his judgment, estimated that a family took in less than 1,000 soles a year, which corresponds to Schaedel's $37 figure. In contrast, my figures show a 1975-76 family income of $633 for Soqa. Money actually entering the campo (much is spent on the coast where it is earned) would be about half the family figure, but still above $300. The three communities of my

---

*Throughout this study Peruvian soles have been translated into U.S. dollars according to the following exchange rates.

August 1976	65 to the dollar
1970-mid 1976	43.8
1965-1969	26.8
1960-1964	27.3

(Dobyns and Doughty 1976: 305)

33

study show the income continuum one would expect
if the economy were indeed being transformed differentially: per capita income for the one community that was able to expand its land base (a
very significant situation, as we shall see) was
a mere $49, while the two other communities showed
figures almost two and a half times as much.

Table 2.1

FAMILY INCOME FOR THREE COMMUNITIES, 1975-76

	Soqa	Pampankiri[a]	Qollu K'uchu[a]
Per capita income	$117	$119	$49
Total family income per year	$551	$491	$237
Family income brought into the community [b]	$314	$342[c]	$162

[a]At the request of my informants, I have given
fictional names to these two communities. The
leaders of Soqa were agreeable that I use this community's true name.

[b]This does not include money spent on the coast.
Compare these figures with Hickman's and Schaedel's
estimates of about $37 for the early sixties.

[c]Higher figure than Soqa reflects the fact that
Pampankiri makes most of its money within the community, by fattening cattle, whereas Soqa earns most
of its money on the coast.

If the amount of money earned is increasing,
then obviously the number of money earners should
also be increasing. A major Catholic University
study (CISEPA 1967: 128) found in a sample of
the Peruvian side of the Titicaca Basin that only
19% of family heads had lived outside their

communities for purposes of seeking work. Ten years later, in Soqa, 74% work on the coast every year or almost every year, while in Pampankiri the figure is 60%.

The amount of purchased family possessions also provides a yardstick of change. A calamina (corrugated metal) roof today costs between $110 and $150 for one edifice of a house complex (usually there are two or three buildings). Calamina, which lasts much longer than the traditional tortora thatch, is an extremely practical status symbol, and one of the first purchases a family makes when it comes into some money. Hickman (1963: 204) found only 10% of his six-community sample possessed calamina roofs. On Soqa today, the average is 1.34 such roofs per family! Similarly, Hickman found that less than half the families in his sample possessed small, pressure kerosene stoves; in Soqa today the figure is 95%. A mere 8% of Hickman's sample had radios; in Soqa, 74% have them.

Another way to measure change is to compare attitudes through time. In 1962, 85% of Hickman's sample agreed or partially agreed that "It is better never to pay money to get food" (ibid: 205). This very strongly suggests the mentality of people living on subsistence agriculture. A mere fourteen years later, only 5% of three communities agreed that it was better never to pay for food.* On a question for which Hickman (pg. 103) found a strong relationship to traditionalism--"Coca and cards tell

*Though I used the same statements as Hickman, he allowed three responses: "agree," "partially agree," and "disagree." I offered only two: "agree" or "disagree." Therefore, our questionnaires are not perfectly comparable.

the truth"--84% agreed or partially agreed. When I presented the same statement to the Soqa sample, only 10% agreed.

By just about any objective measure, it is obvious that most campesinos are no longer on a subsistence agriculture economy, that they are dealing more and more with money, that they are working on the coast more, that their attitudes are becoming more progressive, and that their communities are becoming more open to outside influences.

Why is this happening? More specifically, why is it happening now? It has been suggested (e.g., Pearse 1970; Arrighi 1973; Friedl 1974) that industrialization itself is often the "initial kick" for the transformation of peasant economies. The problem is that in the altiplano there are no industries to speak of. Due to the centering of wealth and industry on the coast, the rural altiplano has been left virtually untouched by Peru's modernization efforts. Of course, opportunities have opened up on the coast, but there have been such opportunities from the turn of the century. Also, if opportunity were the major criterion, we would expect a more or less even migration rate throughout the area, whereas precisely the opposite is the case: in some communities almost no one works on the coast, in others, only a few kilometers away, almost all men work out at least part of the year.

Peruvian industrialization provided a means for the transformation of Aymara economy. It did not provide the stimulus. To understand what is happening today, we must go back centuries, to processes that were set in motion during the early Republican Period.

3. Land, Population, and Positive Feedback

A look at the history of population growth and decline for Peru since the Conquest is highly suggestive. Table 3.1 is based on Colonial, Republican, and modern censuses and, while the first three figures are controversial,* the other figures may be the best available. What we find is a very rapid initial decline, as diseases for which the natives had no defenses take their toll. After 1570 there is a slow growth during the relative peace following Toledo's defeat of Manco Inca in 1572. The slow decline from a peak in 1650 probably reflects the social upheavals and mass deaths of the mita system

---

*Schaedel (1967: 7) holds that the Indian population of the sierra reached pre-Conquest numbers in 1940, which would mean only around six million. Means (1931:269) estimated between sixteen and thirty-two million for the central Andes, preferring the lower number, while Julian Steward (1959: 121) suggested a peak aboriginal population of 3,500,000 for Peru and Bolivia, a figure apparently preferred by Mason (1957: 138). Pike (1957: 7) claims Inca agriculture could not have supported more than eight million, and possibly not more than two or three million--a view I would dispute since many Inca-era agricultural terraces on altiplano hills are now fallow. If all these terraces were farmed, which must have been the case in Inca times, altiplano land could support many more people than it has now.

37

Table 3.1

HISTORIC DEMOGRAPHY OF PERU

Date	Population	% Annual Change
1523	32,000,000	
1530	16,000,000	-7.1
1548	8,285,000	-2.6
1570	2,739,000	-3.0
1650	3,030,000	+0.1
1769	1,076,000	-0.5
1825	2,488,000	+4.5
1836	1,374,000	-3.9
1850	2,002,000	+3.2
1862	2,487,000	+2.0
1876	2,652,000	+0.5
1940	6,208,000	+2.0
1961	9,907,000	+2.8
1972	13,572,000	+3.3

Source: Dobyns and Doughty 1976: 298

and the effects of Tupac Amaru II's 1780 rebellion
that devastated large parts of the country leaving
epidemic after epidemic in its wake. Slowly the
population recoups, only to diminish again during
the innumerable wars that rocked the new nation
after independence in 1824. Only from 1836 does
this fluctuation in population end and the population begin to rise steadily.

Significantly, it was around 1825, during one
of Peru's lowest ebbs of population, that Aymara
ayllu lands were divided among ayllu members and
Spanish inheritance patterns (in which sons and
daughters inherit equally) were introduced. There
must have been, at that time, plenty of land to go
around in the altiplano, not only because of the
extremely low population, but also because

38

immediately after the division of the _ayllus_, most
land holders would have owned similar amounts.
Large differences in landholdings would not yet have
had a chance to develop, and this relative equality
would have meant a surfeit of land for subsistence
for all. In addition, efficiently terraced hill-
sides that are now barren suggest that more land was
productive in the past than today.

Peru's present population is about twelve times
what it was in 1836. If we were to assume that
population grew at a constant rate for all of Peru
and for both urban and agricultural sectors, then
the Soqa family which today works .84 hectares (the
average) would have had at least ten hectares 140
years ago. We really cannot do this, of course, for
several reasons. Altiplano population has grown at
a lower rate than that of the rest of Peru; Carter
(1965a: 20) suggests an increase of 1.5% to 2.0%
per year for the early sixties, compared to a national figure of 2.8%. The urban sector increased much
more than the agricultural sector. And, finally,
these population figures are not sufficiently accurate for any but the most general estimates.

Nevertheless, one fact is obvious: families
possessed more--a great deal more--land in 1836
than do their descendants today. All population
growth has taken place on, at best, a fixed land
base, and this growth was exponential after 1862;
prior to 1940 the population doubled first in sixty-
four years, then in only thirty-two years.

The introduction of Spanish inheritance patterns
around 1824 set in motion a positive feedback process
whereby the number of families owning a given tract
of land at least doubled every generation. For

example, if Eustacio Quispe Phala was sole owner of
a large chacra (parcel of land) and willed it equally to a son and a daughter, the original tract would
then be divided in four, and so on. The sequence
would be 1, 2, 4, 8, 16, 32. . . .   It is not
difficult to see that such a process, when applied
to land holdings, is unstable. So the question is
not, "Why has the system broken down now?" but
rather, "Why did it not break down a long time ago?"

The stabilizing factor is inherent in the very
inheritance rules that over a long period of time
are destabilizing, namely, equal inheritance for
males and females. Going back to Eustacio Quispe,
if his daughter received five hectares and she
married into a family of similar size and wealth
to her own, her husband would inherit five hectares
also. Together they would possess the same amount
of land as their respective parents, though it would
be divided up into twice as many chacras. At
replacement levels of population--that is, two
progeny per family--individual tracts are divided
exponentially but total land holdings per family
remain the same.

Diminishment in the quantity of land per family
only takes place when there are more than two children in each family. Today in Soqa there are about
2.7 living children in each family. This .7 is
responsible for the diminishment in land per family;
he is certainly not so imposing a fellow as to
destroy the Aymara economy very quickly.

We can now understand why (1) there are so
many and such small chacras, and (2) the diminishment of land per family has been slow. But it is
in the nature of a positive feedback system that it

can remain stable for a long time and break down
very quickly.

The most popular example of this is world
population: if the doubling factor--the time necessary for the population to double--keeps getting
shorter, we might reach the point where population
doubles in just ten years, creating such pressures
on resources that the world economic system collap-
ses. For Peru as a whole, exponential population
growth has no predictable relation to land, because
new crop lands on the coast and in the jungle are
constantly being opened up. But such growth
in the altiplano has a direct and inverse relationship to land, because the land base is fixed (or,
worse, diminishing). No new lands will open up in
the predictable future. Thus, as every action
requires and equal and opposite reaction, exponential
population growth in the altiplano means exponential
decline in land per capita, as Figure 3.1 shows.

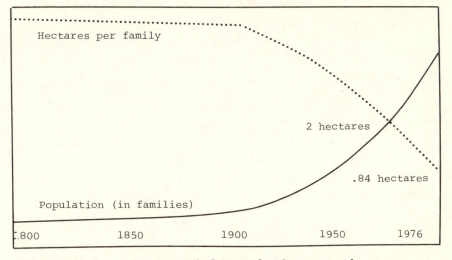

Figure 3.1   Exponential population growth on a
             fixed land base

41

If there is a maximal number of people who can be sustained by subsistence agriculture alone, and if there is a minimal amount of land by which people can so sustain themselves, these would be represented by the point of intersection of the two lines on the graph.

The model reflects reality. It is not clear exactly how much land is necessary to sustain an average family of nearly five people. This depends on the type and quality of land and on the availability of _tortora_. The only professional estimate I have, from an agronomist working in the area around Juli, is a minimum of two hectares. If this is the case, then the line was crossed for many communities some time ago. The 1967 CISEPA study (112-113) gives 1.85 hectares as the average for the Peruvian side of the Titicaca Basin. The Instituto Indigenista Peruana study (1968: 130) gives 1.6 and 1.2 hectares for two communities. The Soqa average is .84 hectares, with 59% of families reporting but half a hectare or less.

The system has tended to favor families who, over time, have had fewer children live to inheritance age. Small differentials in birth and survival rates have, during more than a hundred years, resulted in large differences in land holdings. On Soqa, some report as low as .05 hectares, while others report as much as four hectares under cultivation.

The land-per-family line on our model does not stop at the bare maintenance level of two hectares, but continues its downward curve. In other words, land continues to be divided even after subsistence agriculture is no longer viable. This is called "overshoot" and is characteristic of positive feedback systems; the factors that caused the system to break down will continue of their inertia for some time after collapse.

This is what is happening in the altiplano. Though further division of the land is illegal and clearly dysfunctional, in most communities the old inheritance rules are still in effect. Despite the recognized land shortage in Soqa, 92% of Soqueños answering my questionnaire continue to hold that land is the best inheritance for sons and daughters.

In sum, two positive feedback processes were set in motion almost simultaneously in the early Republican period--an imposed inheritance system that led to increasing division of the land, and population growth at exponential rates. Since, in the beginning, land per family was large and population small, the situation remained stable for a long time, reaching the point of destabilization and collapse suddenly.

Many of the Aymara can no longer live off the land. We will now examine the means by which they have adjusted to this situation.

4. Options and Strategies

With the diminishment of the land beyond the point that a family could subsist, even minimally, by agriculture alone, the Aymara were faced with the problem of finding alternative means of survival. Several possibilities were open: permanent migration to the coast, circular migration, cattle fattening for profit, playing in bands, working at home at some salable craft, migrating to the jungle, or forming land cooperatives.

Many of these were never seriously considered. Fiercely independent as they are, the idea of forming cooperatives is anathema to most of the campesinos with whom I talked, and in Soqa only 4% preferred this as a solution to the land problem. Migration to the jungle is risky; those Aymara who have tried to settle the selva have not usually fared well in such an extremely different agricultural zone, and government support has not been extensive, either in building roads or in providing transportation and aid during the crucial first years. Other options, such as playing in bands, making crafts, or commercial fishing, can be the answers for only a few. Growing crops for market is not a viable option; the family can provide more sustenance growing for its own use than by selling or bartering in the market.

As a rule, that option will be chosen which (1) least disrupts the existing socio-economic system, and (2) causes least trauma for the individual. If only the system itself were involved, permanent migration of the overload population would be an obvious solution, but this is actually an unpopular means of adaptation. While permanent migration may not seriously disrupt the social system, it is most disruptive for the individual, and the individual is claiming priorities. Nevertheless, some do migrate, possibly as high as 14% of adult males in Soqa and 9% in Pampankiri.* Also, the population distribution chart for Soqa (see Appendix) shows a sharp drop between the ages of thirty-one and thirty-five, perhaps reflecting migration in this age group. Permanent migration, however, is such a traumatic repudiation of one's home, culture, and land that, in most cases, we would not expect this option to be chosen as long as less traumatic options were available.

Thus, for the vast majority, the options selected are cattle fattening and circular migration, as Table 4.1 shows.

---

*These figures were arrived at by the very rough means of comparing ages of adult sons, as listed on the census, with adults actually living there. This method of estimating would only be valid with a near 100% sample, viz., those for Soqa Adventists and for Pampankiri.

Table 4.1

FAMILY INCOME EARNED BY VARIOUS MEANS (1975-76)

	Soqa	Pampankiri	Qollu K'uchu
Work outside the community (circular migration)	$397(.72)[a]	$190(.39)	$155(.65)
Cattle sales (bulls and cows)	$124(.23)	$291(.59)	$ 67(.28)
Professional music (fiesta bands)	$ 28(.05)	$ 00(.00)	$ 10(.04)
Market of agricultural produce and crafts	$ 2(.003)	$ 10(.02)	$ 5(.02)
TOTALS	$551	$491	$237

[a]Fraction of total income

AGRICULTURE

Before looking at the alternatives to agriculture, we need to examine this form of livlihood. While diminishing in importance each generation, this remains the principal source of food for most campesinos.

A family's land is seldom concentrated in one place. A wife can inherit land some distance from her new home, so land, even within a single family, may be broken up and widely distributed. Campesinos see this as a benefit, insofar as a local frost or hail will not destroy all of one's crops. A chacra on Soqa may range from five to ten square meters up to 2,000 square meters. A previous study of Soqa (Carmona 1967: 18) showed that family

46

holdings varied from one or two chacras to twenty
or thirty. Two inland communities reveal a variation of from four to 134 chacras per family, and
from one to twenty chacras (IIP 1968: 130). CISEPA
(1967:132), the most comprehensive of these studies,
gives an average of 4.5, with a 1.3 kilometer median
distance between farthest separated chacras.

Altiplano crops are generally restricted to
tubers and grains. Potatoes and two other potato-
like roots, oca and isaño, are the most grown crops.
Barley and some wheat is grown, in addition to two
indigenous and highly nutritious grains, quinoa and
cañihua. About the only green vegetable grown is a
type of broad bean, similar to the lima bean. The
CISEPA study (1967: 112) calculated proportions
for the Titicaca Basin:

Potatoes	.26
Barley	.25
Quinoa	.24
Cañihua	.10
Wheat	.04
Beans and others	.11

Actual quantities vary from community to community.
Soqa, for example, does not grow much quinoa or
cañihua; possessing no pasture land, Soqeños must
always consider yield for cattle feed, and neither
of these crops are competitive with, say, barley or
broad beans. It should be noted that there is no
mention of maize, which is available in markets,
usually as a sugared pop corn, but which does not
grow above 10,000 feet. Onions, which are grown
widely as a cash crop in Bolivia, are never grown
on Soqa, nor are carrots, though both are readily
available in the markets. Onions were virtually a
staple for my every meal in Soqa.

With one crop a year and no refrigeration or canning, some means of preserving foods is absolutely essential. Chuño, a type of freeze-dried potato, has been the answer probably since pre-Inca times. Chuño is made in July or August when freezing weather can be expected. Small potatoes are spread evenly on a flat area of ground, and the family stamps on them all day with a twisting step to break the skins and remove the water. The potatoes are then left to freeze for several nights. I have heard the taste of the resulting chuño described by gringos variously as like cork, cardboard, or blotting paper. The natives seem to like it well enough, however, and use it for almost every meal after September, when most of the fresh potatoes are used up. Chuño will last for years, an important consideration for people who could otherwise not survive a single year's drought.

The agricultural cycle begins with the first spring rains, generally in September but sometimes as late as the middle of November. Wheat, beans, quinoa, oca, and isaño are planted at this time, followed in November and December by potatoes and barley. In January and February there are periodic weedings of potatoes and oca, the pulled weeds being fed to the cattle. Harvest begins in March, in no set order, though, generally speaking, what was sown first will be ripe first. April and May are the principal harvest months, when people work morning to night in the fields, and set up grass or tortora huts to stay in the more distant fields and to guard their crops. June and July are the post-harvest months, when the crops are prepared for eating; wheat and barley are beaten with sticks to

separate the grain from the chaff, and in July
chuño is made. June to September, between harvest
and planting, is the period when houses will be
built, public works will be initiated, and when
marriages and fiestas are most popular. It is
also during this period when the earth is aerated
and made receptive to the rains by plowing.

For sowing, a yunta of two uncastrated bulls is
used to pull an entirely wooden plow or a wooden
plow with a metal tip. The man handles the plow
while women follow in the rows spreading the seed.
Harvest is also a family affair, and is done by
hand or with a cutting implement formed by a piece
of tin tied to a stick and sharpened every few
minutes on a rock. Such tools as the threshing
stick, adz-hoe, clod-crusher, and digging stick
are probably pre-Columbian in origin.

Chacras are never allowed to go fallow, but
crops are rotated on a five-year schedule. Dried
animal feces are gathered and saved throughout the
year to be used as fertilizer or, more simply, a
burro or other animal is tied in the field to be
fertilized. Commercial fertilizers are also sometimes used.

The degree to which agriculture in the altiplano can be improved is debatable. Campesinos are
already highly sophisticated farmers, as shown by
their high yields at an altitude and in a climate
that would intimidate the best of low-country
farmers. One agronomist I talked to, who had
visited the altiplano briefly, felt the Aymara had
already approached the limits of food production,
so there was little further potential. Machinery,
he felt, would be disastrous, because it would cause

49

mass unemployment without significantly increasing the yield. Also, tractors do not produce manure, and commercial fertilizer is expensive. Another agronomist, who had been working with the experimental farm in Juli for some months, believed the yield could be increased. If sufficient drainage is allowed to prevent salt deposits, irrigation from the slightly saline lake might boost crops of present chacras and open up areas now given over to ichu grass. Also, tractor plowing would be better for potatoes, which should be planted deeper than animal plows can reach, though bull-plowing is probably better for quinoa and beans. Without massive government inputs of money, anything large-scale in the way of irrigation, machinery, or commercial fertilizing will not be accomplished. Since 85% of the population, virtually the entire campesino class, produces for itself, with no specialization and with a surplus only sufficient for distribution within the department (CISEPA 1967: 114), it is doubtful that the national government will be stimulated to put much money into the agricultural sector of the economy.

THE MINOR OPTIONS: FISHING, MARKETING, MUSIC

Fishing is economically important for a few, and, in terms of health, for many, as it supplies some of the protein missing from the daily diet. Unfortunately, there are no longer a great many sizeable fish in Lake Titicaca. According to missionary informants, a number of years ago two German canneries opened on either side of the lake, and encouraged fishing by any means, including dynamite, so that the lake was virtually cleaned out over a five-year period. The companies have long left the area, abandoning the empty shells of their plants and warehouses to stand as monuments to modern industrial ecology. Today, mostly small fish, from little-finger length to five inches, are caught. The smaller are fried and sold in the markets to be eaten like potato chips. Five- or six-inch fish are boiled and eaten whole.

Because of the numerous fiestas, playing in brass bands can be a lucrative profession. Though there is status in hiring Bolivian bands, this can cost up to $1,600 for a four-day stint. Peruvian bands charge from $114 to $570, depending on their quality and the distance they must travel. It is possible for an individual, playing from eight to thirty-two fiestas a year, to earn anywhere from $57 to over $400. On Soqa, forty persons play in the island's two bands, bringing in a yearly per-musician average of $421 before expenses (such as instruments and transportation; the alferado, or sponsor, pays all other expenses during a fiesta), a substantial addition to the money economy of the community.

The food markets account for very little income on Soqa. As mentioned, Aymara agriculture remains unspecialized; almost nothing is grown specifically for the market, and most families can easily eat all they can produce. The price of indigenous foods is so low that it is hardly worth the trouble to sell them. Only thirteen people of my Soqa sample of 165 reported selling in the market, and these sold only three or four days a year, so that income from this source brings in merely $21.50 a year for those families involved. Goods would normally be sold only before a fiesta or a marriage, when the family needs new clothes or money to rent dance costumes. This was true in all three communities studied.

For other communities, marketing is an important source of income, and, of course, just about everybody is involved in buying or bartering in the regional markets. Major vendors, those who sell manufactured goods, are mainly from the cholo class; that is, they have left the land and have adopted mestizo clothes and values. Campesinos are involved in small sales of local crops, of bread, of onions and other vegetables, and of fruit brought up from the jungle. They also sell dyes, herbs, and such ritual equipment as llama fetuses, good luck charms, and candies used in rites.

Manufactured goods are paid for with money, while the small-scale sellers, women who sit on the ground with from one to five products spread out before them, will either barter or accept money. Though I have not studied the markets, my impression is that, though barter remains very widespread, money transactions are becoming increasingly common where there used to be barter.

CATTLE FATTENING: THE FIRST MAJOR OPTION

Almost all campesinos raise animals for food, wool, work, or money. On Soqa, where there are no llamas or horses, the average family has 1.3 cows and bulls, 2.9 sheep, .4 pigs, and .74 chickens. Donkeys, which are owned by only a few families, were not counted.

Animals are seldom eaten, except when old or when it is necessary to kill a pig or a sheep to sponsor a fiesta. Cows are raised for breeding and

52

milk, and might be sold when grown, but they are
never, or very seldom, purchased for the sake of
reselling. With bulls the situation is different.

For many communities around the lake, buying,
fattening, and reselling bulls is an important
source of income. For Pampankiri, it is by far the
most important source of money income, and for Soqa
this source is second only to wage labor on the
coast. There are large cattle markets in both Acora
and Ilave. In April through June, campesinos from
communities near the lake buy skinny bulls, bred and
raised in areas far from the lake where there is
poor forage. Campesinos prefer to buy two bulls, a
yunta, so that they can be used for plowing. A bull
bought in June or July for $274 might be sold after
eight to ten months of fattening for $417, giving a
gross profit of $143. Bulls are fed on tortora,
lakeweed, and those parts of the crops that are not
edible by humans, such as the stalks of barley, the
stems of beans, and the above-ground plants of
potatoes and oca. For communities like Soqa, which
has no natural forage, the decision of which crops
to grow is extensively based on cattle-feed yields.

Most communities do not have sufficient cattle
feed for the bulls they buy, and must purchase from
the large tortora fields on the north of the lake
where the famous floating islands of the Urus are
located.* One pichu (bundle) of tortora costs about
34¢, and a single bull can eat three pichus a day,
plus wheat and bean stalks. Qollu K'uchu, which is

_____

*The Urus no longer exist as a separate cultural
group with a distinct language, and the floating
islands (of which the military map shows twenty-
four) are now Quechua and Aymara.

53

away from the lake, needs to buy <u>tortora</u> for daily
feed during October, November, and December, while
Soqa needs buy only occasionally and Pampankiri very
seldom. Thus, there is a vast differential in
actual profits, even considering only money paid out
and coming in. Profits can be as low as a mere $52
per bull or as high as more than twice this amount,
depending on the quantity of feed possessed by the
family.

One study, based on extensive conversations
with <u>campesinos</u> in several lakeside communities,
concluded that cattle fattening operated at a significant loss if the price of the owner's feed and
his labor were considered (CIED 1973: 30-32).
However, the discovery and publication of this
material, in comic book form so that it was easily
accessible even to semi-literate <u>campesinos</u>, had
little effect on cattle sales. Since most cattle
purchased in the altiplano are trucked to the coast,
prices are to a great extent determined in Tacna or
Lima. Also, though purchase prices of cattle by
<u>mestizo</u> and <u>cholo</u> middlemen are exploitively low,
<u>campesinos</u> lack the organizational sophistication
to oppose such exploitation, and they have no back-
up funds to sustain them if they were to withhold
cattle from the market. Then, too, the <u>campesino</u>
is not accustomed to viewing his in-community labor
nor his own <u>tortora</u> or barley stems in terms of
money. What he does clearly understand is that
an initial outlay of money in purchasing skinny
cattle will be increased, in some cases almost
doubled, ten months later, though perhaps with some
further expenditure for feed. I was assured by
informants that for many years cattle fattening was

the only way to become wealthy. Even today it is considered a good enough investment that a number of people on Soqa take out loans every year or every few years to buy more cattle.

Cattle fattening is the least disruptive method of adapting to the diminishing land base, both for the community and for the individual. Accordingly, in the area in which I worked it was universally the first means chosen for entering the money economy on a large scale.

Table 4.2

CATTLE FATTENING IN THREE COMMUNITIES (1975-76)

	Soqa	Pampan-kiri	Qollu K'uchu
Gross earnings per bull	$143	$143	$143
Cost of feed	$ 46	$ 11	$ 91
Profit	$ 97	$132	$ 52
Average number bulls sold per family	1.24	2.19	1.30
Average family income from selling bulls	$120	$289	$ 68
Amount of total family income (does not include occasional sales of cows)	22%	59%	29%

The choice of cattle fattening as the main means of earning money has important bearings on the culture. Cattle fattening brings in money without an excessive effect on the social system. After the initial purchase, one hardly need leave one's chacras. Sowing, harvesting, gathering tortora go on as always. The purchase of cattle introduces little that is new; there is no breach in the boundaries that enclose the community. Thus we would expect that a community, for which this is the major source of income, would remain relatively conservative, that no matter how much money was brought in, the non-economic aspects of culture would remain traditional.

This is precisely the case when we compare Pampankiri, which derives 59% of its income from fattening cattle, with Soqa, which earns most of its income from work on the coast. The former is much more traditional as measured by responses to such questionnaire statements as "The birth of twins signifies a punishment of God" (49% agreed in Pampankiri, 02% in Soqa) or "Machines make men lazy" (Pampankiri 36% agree, Soqa 09%). A community that can fatten cattle can remain a closed community. But such a community is still under the shadow of its growing population, which will ultimately--and soon--pass the limits of what the earth and lake can profitably supply in the way of cattle feed. It is then that a further option must be chosen, then that all of the implications of evolution from a subsistence agriculture economy to a money economy become manifest.

CIRCULAR MIGRATION: THE SECOND MAJOR OPTION

John Donahue (1972: 1) defines circular migration as "the process whereby rural migrants maintain social and economic links with their rural villages

56

or areas of origin and channel resources from the
city back into the rural areas."

Migration is hardly a new institution for the
people of the altiplano, who have a long history of
migratory agriculture to exploit different ecolo-
gical zones. The pre-Inca Lupaca sent migrants to
cotton and maize chacras on the Pacific coast.
The Incas permitted the Aymara to establish colonies
in the jungle and the lower eastern slopes, which
were probably worked by part-year laborers rather
than full-time colonists.

While in the past migration was sporadic and
involved but a small part of the population, today
such movements are becoming the norm for all adult
males in some communities. As early as around 1958,
116,000 adults from southern Peru were migrating
annually to the urban centers, the colonization
projects in the jungle, or to other departments.
Only 10,500 of these remained for an appreciable
number of years, and even ten per cent of this group
has returned to their rural homes (Schaedel 1967:
7). In the Tacna barrios (workers' settlements),
78% of migrants travel in the course of a year, 80%
of these returning to their rural homes (Donahue
1972: 9).

Pressure on the land plus availability of jobs
on the coast have been the two principal conditions
in establishing circular migration as an Aymara
institution. The lack of entrepreneurs in the
Titicaca area and the reluctance of government or
industry to invest in the altiplano have assured
that few jobs are available within the department
of Puno. Rising expectations, especially desire
for goods that can only be purchased with money,

have stimulated migration as earlier migrants bring back radios, bicycles, sewing machines, factory-loomed fabrics, and even motorcycles.

Given an availability of jobs in several locations, the principal factor in the decision of where to migrate is accessibility; a specific area in the _sierra_ will predictably funnel most of its migrants to a specific area on the coast or on the Pacific slopes. In the early sixties, Tacna received 80% of its immigration from the department of Puno, and Ariquipa 86% (Schaedel 1967: 8). According to the 1969 census, in one settlement in Tacna, 82% came from the department of Puno. Between 1955 and 1961, Tacna grew from 10,000 to 25,000, and by 1969 it had doubled to 50,000, largely due to the influx of migrant labor from the _sierra_ (Donahue 1972: 4).

Job opportunities are in farm work, mining, factory work, construction, and dock and railroad loading. Toquepala and Cuajone, a few miles apart, form together the largest open-pit copper mining operation in the world. Ilo, which is the port for exporting the ore, offers jobs not only in loading, but also in construction, as this area is constantly expanding. Tacna is the center for factory labor and the jumping-off point for jobs in the surrounding area.

Jobs in industry are far more lucrative than those in farming, but because mining, construction, and manufacturing companies require contracts, usually of ten to twelve months, workers must stay longer periods away from their altiplano homes, and often must pay relatives to work their land. If such a worker spends an average of more than six months of every year on the coast, he might well keep a second wife and family there; this not only allays loneliness and the disorientation of migration, but also provides better economic contacts and supplies legitimacy in a hostile environment.

These longer-term migrants can earn considerable amounts of money. One migrant who worked in a machine shop in Ilo reported earning $55 a week, plus $27 a month for cost of living, which, if this person worked every week, would add up to over $3,000 a year. This worker reported bringing back to Soqa 50,000 soles.* This, however, is exceptional. Others reported bringing back from $68 after three months to $342 after nine months.

Jobs in industry, however, are sharply limited. Mines, factories, and construction companies have less turnover of workers than farms because of their contracts. Also, some occupations are controlled by syndicates with limited membership. Even applying for such a job might require "knowing someone"--that is, being part of an information network system. These higher-pay, long-term, high-demand jobs could never provide sufficient opportunities for all those seeking work.

Thus commercial farms are by far the most important source of jobs for natives of the altiplano. Government irrigation projects in the riverine valleys and coastal alluvial areas have opened up large regions to commercial farming. The rice chacras at Camana and nearby Tambo are the

_____

*The money earned on the coast would have been at 43.8 to the U.S. dollar. However, he returned just after devaluation to 65 to the dollar, so his 50,000 soles was worth $769, not $1,142.

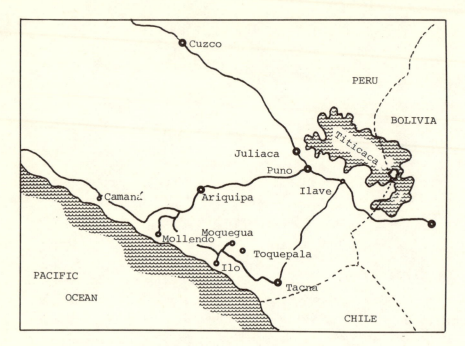

Figure 4.1.   Major centers for circular migration
                from the altiplano.

major sources of work for Soqa. With roughly a two-
month planting season, a two-month first harvest,
and a two-month second harvest, it is possible to
work up to six months in this area, though few work
more than four months. The work situation is similar to that of migrant labor in the United States.
The various companies bid for labor, offering pay
according to the labor available, plus yapas
(bonuses) of pisco (a Peruvian liquor), wine, and
bags of rice. Most workers put in an eight-hour
day, six days a week, though some prefer to join
groups that contract to work a specific area, and
these will work from first dawn until dark every
day until the job is finished. Most live--"like

60

Table 4.3

CIRCULAR MIGRATION IN THREE COMMUNITIES

	Soqa	Pampan-kiri	Qollu K'uchu
Household heads who work outside the community	.74	.60	.36
Types of work (proportion of workers)			
Farm	.74	.83	.38
Construction	.21	.04	.48[a]
Factories, mining	.10	.03	.00
Types of work (Average months per year for one worker)			
Farm	3.9	3.5	1.5
Construction	7.2	1.5	2.0
Factories, mining	10.0	1.5	0.0
Places of work (fraction of workers; includes multiple reportings)			
Ilo	.17	.00	.05
Moquegua	.26	.01	.14
Camana	.65	.81	.00
Tambo	.22	.00	.00
Ariquipa	.03	.01	.10
Tacna	.00	.07	.33
Others (mostly in the altiplano: Puno, Ilave, Juliaca, etc.)	.04	.09	.35

[a]Qollu K'uchu's high rate of construction jobs represents mostly low-pay, short-term jobs in Ilave or Puno, not the contract construction jobs on the coast.

animals," one informant said--in worker shacks belonging to the farm.

At $3.42 to $4.10 a day, the wage in 1975, a worker could expect to earn from $251 to $320 in three months. However, because of transportation and living expenses, insurance deductions, and, in many cases, the cost of liquor and women, only $23 to $91 of this comes back to the altiplano.

After the first trip, migration to the coast is not generally overly traumatic. Many go down in groups; others, even though they may go alone, can step into well-established family or community networks. Just as school has offered children a welcome break from the drab, cheerless childhood of earlier times, so circular migration has offered men an escape from the monotony of the agricultural cycle. CISEPA (1967: 441-442) found that most who had worked outside their communities were satisfied with their jobs and looked forward to returning. They also found that temporary migrants were the most modern and progressive segment of the campesino class.

The progressiveness of migrants is to be expected. These people have temporarily moved out of a closed, traditional society into an open, modernizing society. Some have "city girl" second wives. For part of each year they must speak mostly Spanish, must sustain themselves with money, must deal with complex urban situations and with urban people, must adjust their work and leisure to the clock, and must adopt values adaptive to an environment wholly different from that in which they were raised. Little wonder that many return to their communities feeling sophisticated and superior, like soldiers returning from war. Such attitudes pressure other men within the community to try their hands on the coast.

The Aymara are bicultural; they move between two cultures and adopt the values of each according to need. As with their earnings, the Aymara leave the larger part of their modern values on the coast where such values are most appropriate. But, also as with their earnings, they bring back a small per cent of these values into the community. They desire manufactured goods, education, and modern medicine. They may look askance at their old religion or unthinkingly find it less and less relevant to their lives. The world beyond the community boundaries was a hostile and shadowy place; now it is a known quantity, laden with humiliations, but also with opportunities.

Yet campesino they remain. They are still peasants in the sense that they are consciously and willfully bound to their land and their communities and, generally, to extremely traditional wives and families. Unlike cholos, they have not repudiated their heritage or its symbolic manifestations--its rites, its dances, its dress, its language--and they view themselves as embedded within the ages-old continuity of Aymara culture.

STABILITY AND CHANGE IN THREE COMMUNITIES

A comparison of the three communities in which my questionnaire was given reveals a great deal of differentiation, but along a single line of evolution. One community has hardly entered the money economy; a second community has a fairly high per capita money income, but remains traditional; Soqa has entered the money economy by a route that demands progressiveness.

Qollu K'uchu has a per capita income of $49 per year and a family income of only $237, both figures considerably less than half the incomes of either of the other two communities studied. This does not mean that the people are poor relative to these other communities; it means only that Qollu K'uchu has not run out of land. This community of about one hundred families is situated well away from the lake, pressed against the slopes that rise abruptly to a series of plateaus. Since they are not bounded on one side by another community, they have been able to purchase land from one of the sprawling haciendas, devoted mainly to llama and alpaca raising, that dot the plateau country. Thus they have been able to remain on subsistence agriculture longer than the vast majority of communities, which are completely surrounded by other communities. Only 36% of the men of Qollu K'uchu work outside the community, and many of these accept only short-term local jobs, in Puno or Ilave, averaging less than two months work per person each year. Qollu K'uchu lacks tortora, so must buy cattle feed for entire months at a time; thus it fattens fewer cattle and sells them for less profit than communities near the lake.

In terms of progressiveness, Qollu K'ucheños present an ambiguous picture. They are extremely traditional, as measured by several questions designed to gauge this factor (see Table 4.4), yet they are acutely aware of the changes around them. They fully realize that subsistence agriculture is no longer a viable option (Question 17), but they have no desire to return to their traditional past.

Table 4.4
TRADITIONALISM:
ANSWERS TO SELECTED OPINION QUESTIONS

	Soqa	Pampan-kiri	Qollu K'uchu
8. Machines make men lazy.			
Agree	.09	.36*	.97
Disagree	.91	.58*	.03
9. Coca and cards tell the truth.			
Agree	.10	.46	.22
Disagree	.84	.53	.78
15. The birth of twins signifies a punishment of God.			
Agree	.12	.49	.93
Disagree	.86	.50	.05
17. It is better never to pay money to obtain food.			
Agree	.08	.07	.02
Disagree	.92	.92	.97
20. To have a better life, we must return to the traditional life of our ancestors.			
Agree	.02	.18	.00
Disagree	.97	.80	.97

*Figures to not at up to 1.00 in every case, since "no responses" are not included.

Despite its traditionalism in terms of superstitions and attitudes toward machines, Qollu K'uchu
showed the strongest favorable attitude toward
schooling, an attitude bordering on blind faith.
This results mainly from the extremely heavy influence of the Seventh Day Adventists; perhaps 35%
to 40% of the population belong to this denomination.
The Adventist school was established in the second
decade of this century. While the average of
reported attained grade levels for Qollu K'uchu--
3.98 grades for men and 2.43 for women--is not
believable, it is undoubtedly inflated because of
the virtual worship of education reflected in Table
4.5. As one Qollu K'ucheño told me, "We are out of
land now. We must go out of the community to work,
as the people around us have done for years. Out
there, education is our best hope." This is not an
entirely realistic attitude. The worker on the
coast learns very quickly what education can and
cannot do. Qollu K'uchu may change some of its
opinions once those opinions have been tested
against the reality of migrant labor in the rice
chacras in Camaná.

Qollu K'uchu is like an island in a river, im-
mobile in the current that is carrying everything
else rapidly into the future. Its people are now
gazing at the water, preparing for the big jump, and
if they remain a bit naive about what will be required of them, they will certainly learn fast
enough as soon as they get wet.

The people of Pampankiri have plunged into
the money economy, with a per capita income about
the same as Soqa's, but they are doing everything
they can to swim against the current. With almost

66

Table 4.5

EDUCATION: ANSWERS TO SELECTED OPINION QUESTIONS

	Soqa	Pampan-kiri	Qollu K'uchu
A. What is the most important objective in life?			
1. To earn a lot of money.	.38	.23	.03
2. To give one's children a good education	.17	.19	.86
3. To enjoy life.	.45	.37	.07
4. To earn the respect of the community.	.00	.20	.03
B. If you had at this time 10,000 soles to spend as you wish, how would you spend it?			
1. Give a fiesta.	.01	.04	.02
2. Feed the family.	.67	.34	.27
3. Buy cattle to fatten and sell.	.20	.45	.08
4. Educate your children	.08	.14	.39
5. Invest in a business, such as a shop.	.02	.26	.15
E. The best inheritance for one's children is:			
1. Education	.06	.04	.92
2. Land	.92	.43	.07
3. Money	.01	.53	.02
10. By means of education, one can make of oneself that which one wants.			
Agree	.51	.82	.98
Disagree	.47	.11	.00

60% of their money income from cattle fattening, they have been able to continue largely as agriculturalists. Though 60% of household heads work outside the community each year, almost all of this work is in short-term farm labor. In addition, Pampankiri has had no Protestant influence to speak of, and the native Catholicism is notoriously conservative. Thus the people remain traditional, and were the only group in the three-community sample to significantly give affirmative responses (18%) to the statement, "To have a better life, we must return to the traditional life of our ancestors."

In spite of its remoteness from market centers or major roads, Soqa is not only progressive relative to the other two communities studied, it is probably one of the more progressive and ambitious communities on the western side of the lake. It is the only community I know which has taken on the enormous expense and responsibility of trying to make itself an official villa, or subdistrict (see next chapter). It is more progressive, better educated and wealthier than many communities more advantageously situated.

Seventy-two per cent of Soqa's income is derived from work outside the community. With the majority of families possessing half a hectare or less--and with the tortora chacras that line two sides of the triangular island pressed to their limits for cattle feed to the extent that most families purchase tortora part of the year--Soqa is not able to sustain itself even by a combination of agriculture and cattle fattening. Though the average family fattens and sells 1.24 bulls a year, this source accounts for only 23% of the island's income. Playing in bands provides good money for the island's forty musicians, but such income accounts for a mere five per cent of total community income. Because of the near-complete lack of agricultural surplus, and the distance to the nearest major market, in Acora, income from market sales is negligible.

In regard to attitudes, Soqa rates by far as the least traditional of the three communities in which the questionnaire was given.

This may be partially due to the Adventists who brought primary education to the island in 1914. However, Qollu K'uchu, which had an even more profound Adventist influence, remains relatively conservative. The primary cause of Soqa's progressivism is the high number of people that work on the coast. Thirty-one per cent of these work at long-term jobs in construction, factories, and mining--compared with only nine per cent for Pampankiri.

There is an inverse relationship between Soqa's land and her progressiveness, which may have some general application to other communities. All things being equal, less land leads to more progressiveness. Such an equation can never be very precise, because a number of other factors are also related to progressiveness: Protestant influence, proximity to cities and towns, degree of governmental intervention through such agencies as SINAMOS, how early or late schools were founded in the community, and the orientation of the community leaders. However, availability of land remains the single most important consideration.

If Soqa has entered the money economy more rapidly and more completely than surrounding

communities, we find there not so much an anomaly as
a picture of the future.

BEYOND ECONOMY

It is a truism in anthropology that if change is
fundamental, it will not remain confined to one
sector of the socio-economic system. Change in the
economic sector may have repercussions on religion,
social structure, government, ideology, and population growth. This is certainly true for the Aymara.
In the following chapters I will attempt to document
the various ways in which the economic transformation
is effecting substantial change in several non-
economic subsystems.

5. The Changing Social Structure

A 1967 Catholic University study of a number of communities around the lake found them far more organized than had been believed, with groups of <u>patronatos</u> <u>escolares</u> (patrons of the schools), cooperatives, trade unions, recreational organizations, and religious associations (CISEPA 1967: 159-166). While Soqa lacks trade unions or cooperatives, it is highly structured along a number of different, but overlapping, lines. There are kin groups and ritual kinship relationships, work groups--both kin oriented and community oriented--strong bonds of religion among Seventh Day Adventists, as well as sports groups. In addition, there is a certain hierarchy based on status and wealth, and a complex and well-functioning governmental structure.

As quickly as many traditional ties--such as the extended family as the basic social unit--break down or are weakened under the impact of the economic transformation, new structures develop to replace them. The Aymara system, once believed to be extremely rigid, has turned out to be quite malleable, as the functions of traditional structures are shifted to entirely new structures.

71

STRUCTURES BASED ON RECIPROCITY

Most kin and communal ties are formed by a
system of mutual obligations that permeates almost
every aspect of social life, so that one might well
designate reciprocity as the glue that holds the
society together.

Reciprocity is most evident within family and
kinship relations. When Tschopik (1951: 160) studied in Chucuito in the early forties the patrilineal
extended family, which for centuries had been the
basic unit of Aymara social organization, was still
intact and was just beginning to break down. As we
have seen, the change that Tschopik glimpsed in its
incipient stages has proceeded with such rapidity
that today the nuclear family is the basic unit.
However, kin ties remain strong, especially with
one's parents and with uncles and aunts on either
side. Obligations among relatives include help with
food if there is a bad crop (but never the giving of
land), taking care of orphaned children (a job fall-
ing to either the paternal or maternal uncle), sometimes lending money without interest, and help in
aini.

Aini refers to a type of reciprocal personal
labor (as distinguished from collective work for the
community), such as building houses or working
chacras, but, by extension, the term is often used to
designate just about any form of direct reciprocity.
Aini work groups are fluid, with various friends and
neighbors taking part as available, but close relatives, including fictive kin, are obligated to
participate. Repayment must not always be in kind,
but it must be equal. If a poor man works a richer

72

uncle's chacras, he may be repaid with use of the uncle's burro.

As the community enters the money economy, the aini is losing importance. I have seen campesinos pay in cash for help during harvest, though there still remains sufficient stigma attached to this that it is denied that this is ever done. Aini is also weakened because a large part of the male labor force is away on the coast during the months between harvest and planting, the traditional time for major collective labor projects.

The marriage process is a significant contributor to community cohesion. It was long believed that trial marriage was common among the Aymara, but most anthropologists now agree that this never really existed. Rather, marriage is sequential and progressive. This type of marriage involves a series of rituals in which an inheritance feast, a planting ritual, and a house roofing are as crucial as the formal wedding. Each stage in this process is more binding than the previous stage, not only for the espoused, but also for the couple's families, and for the couple and the community.

Compadrazgo, or godparenthood, alliances are often as strong as blood or marriage relationships. Each person receives three padrinos thoughout his or her life: one at baptism, one at the first haircut, and one at marriage. The padrino has the obligation to help raise and protect his ahijado (godchild), to buy gifts on various feast days, keep the child in clothes, and arrange for schooling. In return, the ahijado, once grown, has the obligation to work for the padrino at the latter's request and at minimum wage. Both Adventists and Catholics, males and females, receive _padrinos_.

Just as there is an increasing tendency to seek _mestizo_ _padrinos_ who will provide contacts in the world beyond the community, so many traditional ties are losing importance or changing form under pressures from entrance into the money economy. Entirely new ties are coming into being, cross-cutting family ties and unifying members of the community that would otherwise have only the most tenuous relations. The strongest of these institutions, for a small percentage of families, is Seventh Day Adventism, which unites a group of people through all-day religious services, socials, and a certain elitism. The Catholics have not been able to form in a similar manner, and the various fiesta dance groups, rather than providing a wider network of relations, overlap existing _aini_ and family groups. Similarly, the _patronatos_ _escolares_--fathers who oversee the schools--form a much tighter and stronger group among Adventists than among Catholics.

Aside from the government, the only group which draws members from all religions and all sectors of the community is the Centro Cultural Deportivo de Soqa, which belongs to the league of sports for the district of Acora and organizes soccer games among the four island teams and all-star games with other communities. The significance of the popularity of soccer should not be underestimated. Not only do the teams form tight bonds of friendship among their members, but the game itself provides more national integration in some ways than government or the market system. A _campesino_ who might be hard pressed to name the Prime Minister of Peru would probably be able to list every major soccer team in the country and would certainly know the most recent opponent of Alfonso Ugarte, the professional Puno team.

Another new bond that has formed only recently is that of groups who travel to the coast together to work. Those who work the rice chacras on a contractual basis may form strongly bonded semi-permanent work groups, while wage workers may make good friends who they would hardly know within the traditional community structure.

CLASS AND STATUS

Class stratification on the altiplano as a whole is so rigid that Tschopik (1951: 159) referred to it as "caste-structured" rather than "class-structured." Present economic changes have by no means broken down these barriers; the gulf that separates campesinos from mestizos is still very wide and very deep.

However, the intermediate class--the cholos--is rapidly growing as land holdings become so small that they may be abandoned, and with them the larger part of campesino culture.

Within the campo there is little class differentiation--all are campesinos--but there is a great deal of status differentiation. Today the path to high status is not, as in Tschopik's (1951: 169) time, via wealth. This may be surprising, since one might think that entrance into the money economy would increase the value of money in regard to status. Yet rarely did any of the 353 respondents to my questionnaire identify the "most important" person in the community with "the richest" person. In fact, there seems to be a very strong myth of equality, so that one is often told, in the face of blatant evidence to the contrary, that no one is any wealthier than anyone else. Those selected as "most important" were virtually all community leaders or those who had made good outside of the community (as was the case with a regularly named Catholic priest who was born and raised in Soqa). In two communities the president was regularly named. In the third community, which does not have a president, people were named who had sufficient education to collaborate with authorities on paperwork and legal work growing out of becoming a comunidad reconocido. The common denominator of status seems to have become the willingness and capacity to deal with the outside world for the good of the community.

AYLLU AND COMMUNITY

If ties of kinship, aini, religion, and soccer informally bind the community into a series of overlapping networks based on reciprocity and social relations, the present government is a formal and highly structured system that not only organizes the people of the community but also provides connections with the outer world.

The traditional form of government, since time immemorial, has been the ayllu. There is some dispute whether the original ayllus were composed of interrelated families (Pike 1957: 8) or unrelated families (Tschopik 1946: 539), but in either case these families lived on a clearly delimited area of land which was semi-communal, to the extent that yearly or periodically land was redistributed according to need as defined by family size. The only land privately owned was that upon which the family

76

house was constructed. Much labor was done in communal groups. The leader of an ayllu, supposedly elected for a year but who in many cases held a semi-permanent position, was the hilacata. He was not only in charge of land redistribution, but also of settling inter-ayllu disputes, judging criminals, and making decisions about crop rotation and irrigation, for which he received a share of crops (Tschopik 1946: 540).

First under Viceroy Toledo and later, and more extensively, by mandate of Simon Bolivar, ayllu lands were divided among the individual families. The ayllu persisted but, as it was no longer bound together by common landholdings and extensive common labor, a series of yearly ayllu-wide fiestas took on this uniting function, a crucial function as some ayllus did not follow the logical limits of geography but were splattered, like spilled water, in all directions. The hilacata took on the job of stewardship of some of these fiestas. This became so expensive that in the Bolivian community studied by Carter (1965a: 60-63), the hilacata incurred considerable expenditures by opening his house to visitors and by paying for several major fiestas. When Tschopik (1946) studied Chucuito, the ayllu system was alive and well throughout the entire area. Today it has virtually disappeared.

The deliberate decision by the people of Soqa to abandon the ages-old ayllu system in 1952 was the first major non-economic response to the diminishing land situation. "We could no longer support all the fiestas," I was told. Soqa's three ayllus--Qollana, Surupa, and Urinsaya--were not confined to the island, as simple logic would have ordained, but

77

flowed across the causeway and into surrounding villages. Holding these haphazard units together required innumerable fiestas at great expense, and since these expenses were not in money but in produce, the diminishment in land per family had a telling effect. While it is true that such fiestas acted as redistributive systems, they also required large, short-term expenditures in agricultural goods and animals for people who could no longer support even their own families on available land.

Nor were ayllus adaptive to the new world into which the Aymara were moving. They were closed systems, which had assumed their post-Colonial configuration partially as a defense against mestizo encroachment on the campo. They were protectively organized to keep the mestizos out, and thus offered no paths of communication to district, department, or state governments or to the national market. The new governmental structure, voluntarily adopted in 1952, not only reduced the number and costs of fiestas, bringing them back within the means of the average family, but also opened avenues of communication with the outer world. The men live increasingly outside their communities, which requires a knowledge of Spanish, of reading, and of elementary math skills. Except for the minority of Adventists, who founded their own schools early this century, these tools had to come from outside--via schools provided by the government. The clinic which Soqa is now building is based on a design supplied by the government, and the finished construction will be staffed once a week or so by government nurses and government-trained health promoters (the missionary-founded health promoter program was being

78

assimilated by the Puno Ministry of Health as I left).

The present governmental structure of Soqa divides the island into six sectors, roughly equivalent in population (boundaries are redrawn if one sector becomes conspicuously more or less populous than the others). The whole is headed by a presidente who, like all other officials, is supposedly voted for a term of one year at an annual meeting for this purpose in January. Actually, there may be no rivals for some or most positions, so a person may hold the same office for several years without challenge. A hundred to two hundred people attend the voting meetings, where voting is by hand. Women can vote, but seldom do; in the last election only about twenty voted. There was no election in 1976.

Community government is divided in two parts, the municipal and the political. The agente municipal heads the municipal side and is directly under the mayor of the district of Acora. He is responsible for roads, plazas, keeping records, etc. He has a secretary, the teniente alcalde, and is in charge of the vigilantes del campo and their auxiliaries, who have the responsibility for chacras, tortora, roads, and public dangers within each of the six sectors. The gobernador teniente is head of the political part of the government, which is mainly concerned with laws, and acts as judge for minor crimes and disputes over land. He is directly under both the governor of Acora and the military commandant of Acora, and through them is recognized by the department of Puno. Under him is a teniente auxiliar for each sector. There is also a Sargento de la Playa (Sergeant of the Beach) who is directly

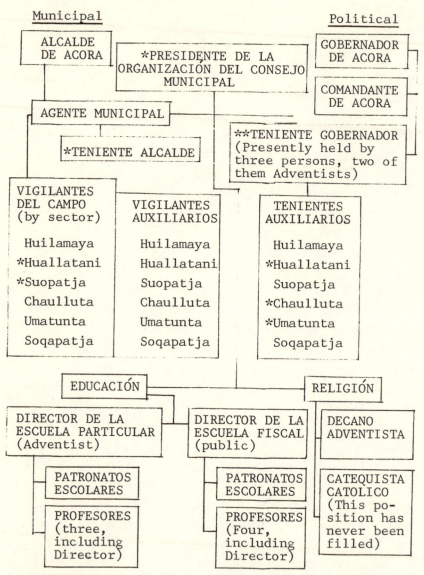

Municipal   Political

ALCALDE
DE ACORA   *PRESIDENTE DE LA   GOBERNADOR
                  ORGANIZACIÓN DEL CONSEJO   DE ACORA
                  MUNICIPAL
                                                 COMANDANTE
   AGENTE MUNICIPAL   DE ACORA

         *TENIENTE ALCALDE   **TENIENTE GOBERNADOR
                                      (Presently held by
                                      three persons, two of
                                      them Adventists)

VIGILANTES
DEL CAMPO   VIGILANTES   TENIENTES
(by sector)   AUXILIARIOS   AUXILIARIOS

Huilamaya   Huilamaya   Huilamaya

*Huallatani   Huallatani   *Huallatani

*Suopatja   Suopatja   Suopatja

Chaulluta   Chaulluta   *Chaulluta

Umatunta   Umatunta   *Umatunta

Soqapatja   Soqapatja   Soqapatja

         EDUCACIÓN   RELIGIÓN

DIRECTOR DE LA   DIRECTOR DE LA   DECANO
ESCUELA PARTICULAR   ESCUELA FISCAL   ADVENTISTA
(Adventist)   (public)

   PATRONATOS   PATRONATOS   CATEQUISTA
   ESCOLARES   ESCOLARES   CATOLICO
                                           (This po-
   PROFESORES   PROFESORES   sition has
   (three,   (Four,   never been
   including   including   filled)
   Director)   Director)

*Asterisk designates Protestant. All are Adventist
except the Vigilante de Suopatja who is the community's only Jehovah's Witness. Only non-religious
positions are so designated.

Figure 5.1   Soqa Political Organization

80

under the Captain of the Port of Puno and has the
authority to enforce laws of fishing, prevent contraband by boat, and can order boats used for community
labor. Finally, there is a community presidente, an
office sufficiently ill-defined to be shaped by the
man who holds it.

The actual center of power is not fixed because
three positions are nearly equal; community control
may lie with the agente municipal, the teniente
gobernador, or the presidente, depending on the
strength of personality of the individuals holding
these offices. On Soqa, it is without doubt the
president who is the directive force in the community.

This is not a small matter: Soqa is going
places. Having rejected any attempt to become a
comunidad reconocido because of the requirement that
such a community have some common lands, Soqa has
set its eye on becoming a villa, or subdistrict.
This is an ambitious project; to become recognized
as a villa, a community not only needs an elementary
school, but also a secondary school, a clinic, a
consejo (town hall), a market, and a plaza with
shops. In the three short years since Soqa was
inspired by its president to become a villa, it has
cleared an area for a plaza, built a two-story
consejo, and has erected the walls of a clinic.

Community meetings are democratic; anyone may,
and does, speak, though the president is obviously
in charge. The meetings, which are called irregu-
larly according to need, take place on a mound of
dirt in front of the consejo. At one of the meetings I witnessed, the agente municipal and teniente
gobernador stood on the mound with the president,

81

but remained silent. Except for the president whose authority was as real as it was official, authority fell more to personalities than to titles, the Sargento de la Playa and the director of the public school acting alternately as second in command. The meeting had been called to convince the people to take a questionnaire given by the school board of the district of Acora. The people did not want to cooperate; they were afraid that it would either be used to impose taxes or to collectivize the land (the questionnaire was still not ready when I left Peru eight months later). A new public school teacher was required to give a speech introducing herself, which she did in Spanish at great length and with considerable arm waving. The speech was accepted with mild applause, after which someone suggested that such speeches would be more meaning-ful if the public school teachers showed up on time and did not take so many days off. The ensuing argument lasted two hours, after which the meeting broke up.

One of the chief functions of the government is drumming up money for community projects and organ-izing collective labor. Aside from the calamina roof, the major expense for the consejo was windows. In order to encourage donations for these, the president promised to have the initials of the donor inscribed in two-foot-high metal figures on each window, a ploy that was quite successful. However, right up until a few days before Soqa Day--cele-brating the community's founding--the men were still too busy with harvest to finish the consejo. This could have proved an embarrassment because a number of officials from Acora and surrounding communities

82

had been invited to Soqa Day festivities. The
president lacks power to tell anyone to do anything.
Therefore, when he thought work should be started
on the consejo, he went up to the unfinished build-
ing--it had walls and a roof--rolled up his sleeves,
and supervised the two men who were making mud and
slapping it on the walls as outer finish. Now and
then someone would happen by, help for an hour or
two, usually in the same supervisory capacity as the
president, and move on. This process continued
for three days, until there were four men working
full time. The suggestion, or intimidation, was
successful. On the fourth day there were perhaps
seventy-five men, on the fifth a hundred-fifty, and
for the two final days perhaps two hundred working
from first dawn until midnight. They were superbly
organized, one group making mortar for windows,
another fashioning rope of ichu grass, another bringing water from the lake, others tying tortora to the
rafters to make ceilings. Within a few days the
empty shell was transformed into a two-story, multi-
roomed consejo, yet unfinished but far enough along
to show off on Soqa Day.

The consejo was a major collective effort. The
roof alone cost over $900, which was donated by
virtually every family on the island. A standing
construction committee for all such works was in
charge of plans and purchases, while sector teniente
auxiliares were charged with collecting donations.
Each sector was responsible for a certain amount
of money (which will ultimately total about $2,300)
and labor.

Another major collective labor job done while I
was on Soqa was the improvement of the causeway.

83

This hundred-yard earthen span is knee-deep under
water during rainy season, and at least ankle deep
well into June. Its dirt surface was continually
being washed away by the flow of lake water. The
idea was not so much to build it up above all
flooding--a job which will only be accomplished over
a period of many years--but to raise it sufficiently
that it will be dry by early summer and to give it
a rock surface. The work was overseen by the construction committee, with each sector ordered to do
a certain amount over a period of months. Soqa's
four wooden fishing boats were required by the
Sargento de la Playa to spend a specified number of
days bringing rocks to the causeway. In addition,
the school patronatos, though not under the authority
of the construction committee, organized the children to spend an entire school day carrying rocks to
the causeway.

Other major public works have included the
construction of the public school, the building of
the walls of the posta, the clearing of the pro-
jected plaza, and the clearing of roads and paths.
The Adventists have just completed a new temple
with a cement floor, high glass windows, and a
calamina roof, and they already have a large school
complex. In addition, Soqueños were involved in the
construction of the road from Acora to Soqa, the
government having required fifteen days per adult
male as a work tax from all communities being
serviced by the road.

The efficiency of the Soqa government is not a
given outcome of the structure of the system, though
this certainly is a factor. The crucial and un-
predictable element in any community is the quality,

ambition, and enthusiasm of the leadership. On
Soqa this leadership has been exceptional, a fact
which points to another crucial effect of the transformation of government structure, namely, the
secularization of government.

The hilacata, by definition, was Catholic, because he was ritual leader as well as official
leader. As soon as the ayllu system disappeared, an
Adventist was voted in as presidente. Today Adventists hold the bulk of political power because
they are better educated to assume the responsibil-
ities demanded by the new governmental structure
with its constant interaction with district agencies.

The change from ayllu to community has not
been without its confusions. When I first visited
the altiplano, I could not ascertain the basic local
unit of government. Some informants said only groups
legally recognized by the government were communities. Non-reconocido groups were ayllus, no matter
what their structure, according to some. Others
said the basic unit was the parcialidad, while some
said this merely designated a sector of a community.
Only on my second visit to Peru was I able to
determine that the disagreement did not derive from
my misunderstanding my informants; the confusion was
common to the campesinos, too. Nor was it a purely
verbal confusion. Where present government structures have only recently been assumed, ayllu loyalties may continue to transcend community boundaries.
I know of two communities on the Ilave Peninsula
that are supposedly sectors of a large community,
but which together function as a single community.
Pampankiri, also supposedly a sector, has the full
governmental structure of an autonomous community.

Soqa, which made the changeover earlier than many, already has the mature and well-functioning modern government that we might expect more transitional groups to assume in the future.

SUMMARY

The Aymara social system was relatively closed in the sense that interpersonal bonds were limited to a few traditional structures: family and kin, aini groups, and ayllu. Even within the community system a number of new relations have recently developed, based on sports, friendships formed from work on the coast, school associations, and bonds related to the new governmental structure. While such groups remain largely within the community system, they are internal responses to inputs from without--such as wage labor, government-supported schools, and a new political structure based on a national model.

More important in the long run are those new relations which transcend the community. Whereas traditional structures, such as the ayllu, were relatively self-sufficient and provided only minimal interaction with the peasant system's wider environment, today on Soqa there are numerous channels of communication with the outside world. The most systematized of these is the government, which has direct lines through its leaders to district officials. Work on the coast provides extensive contact with the once remote industrial world, and undoubtedly results in many extra-community friendships. Even the family is no longer a closed group: teenage sons and daughters are regularly sent to Acora for high school.

The Aymara community system is not, then, the passive recipient of inputs from the wider national system. There are many outputs, such as workers, students, and requests to district agencies. These outputs in turn result in new inputs, as students and workers bring back new skills and values and as political requests are acted upon by the district government (e.g., the recent improvement of the truck road to Soqa). Thus there is a constant feedback, in which outputs lead to inputs and vice versa, which increasingly opens the system.

The "initial kick" that set this process in motion was, as we have seen, the breakdown of the ancient subsistence-agriculture economic system due to population pressure. This means that the process was set in motion not by external forces--such as indusrialization--but by inherently unstable mechanisms within the Aymara peasant system itself.

6. New Functions for Old Religions

There are essentially three religions in the altiplano: the indigenous, the Catholic, and the Protestant. The latter is autonomous of the other two, though Adventists, Baptists, and a smattering of Jehovah's Witnesses may participate in native planting and harvest rites that are pre-Inca in origin. The indigenous religion and Catholicism are generally held by the same people; the two have partially syncretized, though by and large they remain distinct.

Bolton (1973: 254) has noted the extreme "cognitive inconsistency" of Andean peasants, and this inconsistency certainly shows itself in religion. The ordinary peasant is not aware of any coherent theology or system which would unite all of his disparate religious beliefs. Rather, for most, religion is a utilitarian continuum, with the ancient religion at one pole and pure Catholicism at the other, and from which indigenous gods or earth spirits, saints or saviors, can be called upon according to the specific needs of the moment. Thus it might be said that the religion exists more through activity, through the practice of rites and ceremonies, than through a belief system. Indeed, in some places, and Soqa is notable in this respect, Catholicism is virtually equivalent to the fiesta system.

As we might expect, the economic changes which the Aymara are presently undergoing have had their effect on religion. Certain trends are already strongly in evidence.

THE INDIGENOUS RELIGION

Even those who practice both Catholicism and the indigenous religion recognize the difference between the two. On my questionnaire, the majority of Catholics answering found a conflict between "the Catholic religion and the religion of our ancestors." However, it is doubtful if this separation is made in practice, so deeply ingrained are both religions.

The indigenous religion today is probably but a shadow of what it was in ancient times. The Aymara originally possessed some sort of temple cult, with many temples being erected as late as Inca domination. This formal religion, with its priests, places of worship, and public ceremonials was sufficiently visible that it was easily wiped out in post-conquest times, leaving behind a considerable number of popular beliefs.

While sabios (wise men) and some ordinary people might hold a detailed and coherent syncretic theology of the Three Worlds and the powers of each (Ochoa 1974a), for the ordinary man the indigenous religion today is essentially one of spirits that can be controlled by rites. Tschopik (1951: 190) lists a bewildering array of such spirits, which he roughly categorizes--with the recognition that these categories are not held by the people

89

themselves--as "guardians" (household spirits that inhabit dwellings), place spirits, physiological spirits inhabiting lakes, rivers, mountains, etc., meteorological spirits of lightning, hail, and rain, and "owners" that control the food supply and natural resources. The Aymara subsume most of these under the general term achachilla.

In addition, there are a number of demons, such as the supaya that dwell in caves and ruins, a lake monster or monsters called katari, and a severed human head, named qataqate, that flies through the air and sucks human blood. Certainly one of the most interesting, from a gringo point of view, is the karaciti, a dead spirit that walks alone at night and steals the fat of a sleeping person. This spirit is usually that of a Catholic priest-- a symbol too blatant to require much interpretation-- who uses the fat to make candles for mass. It may also be a mestizo or any gringo, the only require-ment being that the karaciti be educated and have books containing the spells used to put people to sleep and steal their fat, which is thought to contain a person's life force. Though an attack can come at any time of the year, August is the month of demons, and especially of karacitis, when mission-aries and others working with the Aymara must take precautions to keep from being accused. Some mis-sionary work in the campo has been ruined because of such rumors. People really do get sick and some-times die from karaciti attacks, which rob the victim of energy so that he slowly wastes away. Given the symptoms, it is probable that such diag-noses may be used in cases of hepatitus and other debilitating ailments, as well as psychosomatic

illnesses. Gringa nurses have told me they have seen
fresh scars, attributed to karaciti attacks, over
the area of the kidneys. One U.S. priest has sometimes cured such attacks with holy water, a paradox
that demonstrates the ambiguity of peasant attitudes
toward foreign priests.

Achachillas are constantly petitioned and
supplicated through rites. These rites, which must
be performed with exactness if they are not to fail
or, worse, bring the punishment of the solicited
spirit, are conducted by yatiris. This is a general
term that subsumes a number of specialists: resiris
who can treat with Jesus and the Catholic saints,
lectors de coca who read coca leaves to divine the
future and to diagnose sickness, thaliris who can
foretell the future by several means (such as
reading the forms taken by melted lead dropped into
cold water), yatiris who can cure, perform protective rites, and divine the future, ch'amacanis who
communicate with spirits, and finally, the paqos
and mesanis who stand at the top of
the hierarchy and can perform all ritual functions.
In addition, there are the laika, the witches of
Manka Pacha (the underworld) who solely perform
rites to hurt or kill enemies. To become a yatiri
one should be struck by lightning or have lightning
strike very near one. These are not uncommon occur-
rences and probably many yatiris really have under-
gone this initiation.

Judging from the extreme utilitarianism of
Aymara religion, it would seem that indigenous
beliefs and rites have functioned largely as a means
of gaining magical control in those areas which are
beyond the pale of volition. Lacking irrigation or,

91

for the most part, chemical fertilizers, tied to
farming methods and tools that date back hundreds of
years, the Aymara remain almost totally subject to
the whims of nature in their agricultural production
and cattle raising. For lakeside communities, the
slightest rise in the level of the lake above normal
can inundate hundreds of hectares of crucial farm-
land and reduce the yearly growth of tortora which,
because its roots need sun, can only grow in a few
feet of water. A drought, on the other hand, can
mean starvation; very few emergency aid rations ever
survive the tortuous path through a corrupt and
bloated bureaucracy (see Dew 1969). Modern medicine has not appreciably entered the campo, even
though the few missionary nurses work to their
capacity.

Little wonder then that ritual, that is, the
utilitarian aspect of religion, clings tenaciously
while the belief system--as a consistent and coherent
theology or cosmogony--has for many people virtually
disappeared. The Adventists on Soqa, though referring to all non-Protestants as "pagans" and to
indigenous Aymara beliefs as "superstitions,"
nevertheless continue to faithfully practice ancient
planting and harvest rites.

Today the older people are the bearers of the
belief system upon which ritual is based, while the
younger generation--brought up in schools which not
only teach Christian religion as a required course
but also teach the various sciences--has only partially assimilated these beliefs. Yet, while the
pagan belief system may be replaced by Christianity
or scientific conceptions without any particular
loss, ritual remains, for the large majority of the

people and in most situations, the only means of
control over weather, sickness, accidents, and
destiny. The schoolbook knowledge of science has
long preceded the influence of technology on the
lives of the people, and Christianity lacks mechanisms to heal the sick or grow the crops or prevent
lightning. The old religion is breaking down, but
it is breaking down differentially. For the large
part, the coherent theology which once provided a
unifying framework for the religion is already gone.
A confusion of minor gods, saints, spirits, and
demons remains, but many of the younger generation
are already expressing doubts or outright abrogation.
Thus the religion is fading in bits, like a great
Cheshire cat, its body--the theological system--
gone; its stripes--the spirits--fading; so that
only the grin of ritual will endure.

But ritual, too, shows at least incipient
signs of dissolving. It is common to hear that
there are far fewer yatiris than in years past, and
in some communities, such as Soqa, it is claimed
there are none. As people take charge of their
lives through work on the coast, rather than relying
totally on agriculture, as commercial fertilizer and
perhaps irrigation come more into use, as modern
medicine enters the campo, control will pass from
the realm of ritual to the realm of technology and
individual volition.

For all the Colonial missionization by the
sword, for all the dedicated priests and nuns and
preachers who have come recently, it may ultimately
be technology and medicine that make Christians of
the Aymara.

CATHOLICISM

"It has been said," observes Tschopik (1946: 509), "that the Aymara were conquered more by the Dominican fathers than by Spanish soldiers." From the arrival of the altiplano's first Dominican missionary in 1539, the Aymara were indeed more "conquered" than "converted," the Dominicans so enriching themselves by exploitation of the natives that other sects became jealous and the Dominicans were expelled. They were replaced in 1577 by the Jesuits who, through estancias and mining, developed Chucuito and Juli into two of the richest cities in Peru, rivaled only by Cuzco and Lima. The Jesuits, in their turn, became too rich and powerful to be tolerated, and in 1767 were expelled from all South America by Charles III.

During this time, priests, euphemistically called "visitors," traveled from community to community throughout Peru, interrogating campesinos under threat of punishment, burning idols, converting en masse to Christianity, and having retrogressors and sorcerers whipped or carried off to prison. One record for the period from February 1617 reveals the criteria of success:

> There were 5,694 confessions; 669 ministers of idolatry were discovered and punished; 603 principal huacas were taken away from them, as well as 3,418 conapas, 45 mamazaras, 189 huancas, and 617 malquis; 63 witches of the lowlands were punished. About 357 cradles were burned, 477 bodies were returned to the church (Arriaga 1968: 2).*

---

*A huaca is an idol or sacred object; conapa, a small sacred object worshipped privately; mamazaros, pottery ears of corn, worshipped as Mother of the

94

To prevent backsliding after the visitor had left, a set of specific regulations were left behind to be enforced, one gathers, by the most zealous of converts; no one should be called by the name of a sacred object or spirit, there must be no planting or harvest festivals, no singing in the native tongue, no drunkenness, no curing by magicians, and no placing of food on tombs. The common punishment for infractions was one hundred lashes and the shaving of the malfactor's head.

Until about 1945 the Church remained remote at best, at worst actively oppressive, certainly always a bastion against any threat to the status quo. As we shall see in the next chapter, the Church vigorously fought campesino education and encouraged mass drunkenness. Altruism, especially if it threatens one's own livelihood or that of one's patrons, is a luxury, and few people in the altiplano could afford luxuries, certainly not priests, who survived on the donations of mestizo patrons and on the payments of campesinos for masses during fiestas.

Altruism had to come from the outside, from a group with nothing to lose and sufficient resources to survive initial failures. The Maryknoll missionaries, based at Maryknoll, New York, and U.S. and Spanish nuns from a number of different orders, have brought that altruism and, in gaining a virtual monopoly on Catholicism in certain areas of the Titicaca Basin, have significantly changed the nature and orientation of the local church. They

---

Corn; huanca, a large stone placed on top of a house to protect it; malquis, the mummy of an ancestor. These are all Quechua terms.

have formed the altiplano's first successful loan
co-op, have overseen extensive innoculation programs,
have run an educational radio station for the Aymara
and presently run two institutes which publish and
disseminate information of value to campesinos, have
developed the successful program of campesino health
promoters, and have constructed roads (e.g., the
original road from Acora to Soqa). They run an
experimental farm near Juli, teach modern farming
methods, teach courses in nutrition, and, in emer-
gencies, distribute food and clothes from the
Catholic relief organization Caritas. Nurses are
too few to significantly change the health situation
on their own, even working themselves to exhaustion
in the campo or in village clinics, but to the many
individuals who have benefited, they must indeed
appear as angels.

This does not mean that the missionaries are
completely accepted or their contribution completely
trusted. Hickman's 1962 questionnaire included the
statement: "The Maryknoll priests are here to deceive
the people." Twenty-seven per cent agreed and an
additional 40% agreed in part (1963: 204). The
situation today would probably be more favorable to
the missionaries, though when I included this same
statement in my test questionnaire, so many people
refused to answer that I left it off the final version. Nevertheless, it is my experience that, while
any outsider will be distrusted, missionaries are
more trusted than government agents or city mestizos.
In fact, if there is a single non-Indian group in
the altiplano that could claim the highest degree of
trust, it would be the missionary nurses. The
Aymara neither understand nor quite believe in

96

altruistic motives, but they do respond to results, and the nurses have provided the most visible of these.

Despite extensive social goals, missionization remains primarily focused on religious work. The stated--and yearly restated--goal of Maryknoll is to create an indigenous church, run largely or exclusively by the Aymara themselves. Though the missionaries have built a seminary in Puno (now used for secular purposes by the government) and spent years training pastors, they are today little nearer their goal than they were three decades ago. A good part of the problem lies in strictures coming from Rome. Celibacy is so utterly meaningless to the Aymara that it is difficult to create an indigenous priesthood, and the Church is so rigidly structured that catechists simply cannot take over this function; the people are acutely aware of the Church hierarchy and refuse to accept a chatechist where they want a padre, or to accept a culta (rite given by a catechist) when they want a mass. More than a dozen priests were ordained from the Puno seminary, but almost all of them deserted the altiplano for more hospitable climes. Unfortunately, the training which makes a priest also makes a mestizo; a campesino priest is a contradiction in terms. Another problem is that the natives simply do not want the foreign priests to leave; gringos possess more magical power than locals.

Unable to form a native priesthood or to attract a majority of natural leaders to become catechists, some foreign missionaries become almost the exact equivilent of parish priests in small-town United States: they give masses, perform

97

weddings and baptisms, visit the sick and prisoners
in jail, conduct money-raising socials, and lead
fiesta processions. Most would agree that these
should be jobs performed by native clergy, but it is
not happening.

One major reason it is not happening is that
people really are not all that Catholic. Escobar
(1967: 55) suggests that the pantheon of saints which
was introduced in order to combat the indigenous cos-
mogony only changed the form and the names of the
polytheism it was introduced to combat. Actually, it
is doubtful that missionization even accomplished
this much. The larger part of the ancient pantheon
has neither been eradicated nor replaced, and though
some of the saints may have taken on certain relation-
ships--Santiago to lightning, San Antonio to animals
--they are largely ignored except as patrons of the
fiestas which bear their names. The organization of
the days of the fiesta, introduced after conquest,
was virtually the only aspect of Christianity to become deeply ingrained within the culture, and this
in a sense that would probably appall the most lib-
eral Vatican prelate. It is difficult to find any
aspect of Christianity that survived intact its
transfer from European to Aymara culture. The Indians have adapted everything to their own needs and
their own mentality and world view. If, in the past,
they have been systematically exploited by the Catholic missionaries on the physical level, they remain
the victors in the battle of ideology. The indigenous popular religion (as distinguished from the
elite temple religion) was enriched by the Catholic
influence.

The ancient shrine of Copacabana, on a penin-

sula in the southern, Bolivian, part of the lake, is
ostensibly Christian. During the week of August 6,
tens of thousands of Aymara come to follow the sta-
tions of the cross up a high hill, on top of which
are a series of large concrete crosses. All very
Christian. Going up the hill one tosses a rock onto
the base of each cross; if the rock stays, it will
be a good year, if it falls, a bad one. Midway on
the hill one builds a house with mud or rocks and
blesses it with liquor to assure getting a better
house in the future. It is lucky to tie ichu grass
in a knot with one hand. Higher up, there is a natural tunnel of rock; if one can pass through he will
survive the year; if he gets stuck, death has grabbed
him and he will die during the year. There is always
a long line in front of this brief tunnel. The air
on top of the hill is thick and brown with incense,
for around the base of every cross are yatiris blessing the people for a price. Farther on are stalls
selling miniature plastic trucks and houses, some
very elaborate, and tiny cans of soup and boxes of
macaroni, anything one could want, in miniature.
To gain the real thing, one must buy miniatures--say,
a house and a truck--take them to an area slightly
down the hill, build a mud wall around the house,
plant a branch as a tree, buy an official title and
have it validified by one of the many abogados (law-
yers) on the hill for that purpose, have a ceremony
with wine (a little on the ground for Pachamama, a
little on the house, a little on the truck, drink a
little and pass the bottle) and perhaps even hire a
yatiri to do the blessing.

   While popular Christianity is largely a development of the Aymara themselves, formal Church

Christianity may seem remote. An altiplano mass
would be celebrated in a huge church built in a style
designed for European cities in the Middle Ages,
would include a ritual created by and for Medieval
Italians having to do with a Jew who lived in the
Middle East two thousand years ago, and officiated
by a gringo from New Jersey speaking in the language
of the Iberian conquerors. What meaning all this
could have for an Aymara campesino is anybody's
guess.

Yet Catholic Christianity may be growing in importance. The pagan religion is functionally bound
to the land, which is diminishing in economic importance as it diminishes in hectares per family. The
Catholic Church, on the other hand, has for centuries
provided virtually the only paths of communication
with the outside world, and has acted as mediator
between the Indians and the mestizos. In colonial
times, Catholic priests were sometimes protective
of their charges, and even when the clergy itself
settled into a pattern of corruption and exploitation
it remained the most accessible representative of
mestizo culture. Today missionaries provide an
altruistic kind of social aid not available from
government sources.

As the Aymara move out of their tight, closed
system into the wider world, their indigenous religion will increasingly fail to offer the support
they need. The Catholic religion can fulfill this
function, but only if it recognizes the need and provides the services required. One pressing need is
for religious sodalities on the coast. Several Protestant groups, notably the Seventh Day Adventists
and Jehovah's Witnesses, are already providing such

sodalities, which offer moral support at the critical moment in lives of many young men down for the first time, and provide valuable centers for information networks to help find housing, gain jobs, and locate relatives. Though the Catholic Church has not been active in this regard, as I left there had already been some discussion of extending the altiplano sphere of influence down the western slopes to Camana' and Tacna. This would be an important move; it would recognize that circular migration has become an institution for the Aymara. Their once-closed world now extends to the Pacific.

Today towns, wage labor, big industry, and the Spanish language are becoming as familiar to many campesinos as their rural communities. The indigenous religion of earth spirits and lake demons has no more meaning here than Christian theology has for the peasant whose life is totally immersed in the yearly agricultural cycle. Christianity, or some peculiar Aymara adaptation, may well be the religion of the future, not because it is truer or more beautiful than the indigenous religion, but rather because it is better adapted to a money economy and all that this entails for the Aymara.

THE FIESTA SYSTEM

While many Aymara will occasionally attend a mass or baptism, and have at least a vague idea of the story of Christ, it is in the fiesta that the Aymara's Catholicism truly finds its expression. For a great number of people, and this includes the majority of Soqueños, the Catholic religion is the fiesta system. A community celebrates a number of fiestas during a year, each from two to four days

101

long. Aside from the nineteen universally celebrated
fiestas de guardar, there are local fiestas, giving
a total of more or less 170 days a year in which one
can celebrate in some part of the department of Puno.

All religious fiestas take roughly the same
form. A hired band or a local flute-and-drum group
follows ten to twenty dancing couples, all in cos-
tume appropriate to the particular fiesta. There is
music and dancing throughout the day, with simul-
taneous drinking of beer and pusitunka*, and occa-
sional stops for drinking. Drunkenness is not something extraneous or "added on" to the basic fiesta
format, but is a crucial and integral part of the
dance experience, and one that children learn early
from observing their parents. At the Campesino Day
festivities in Acora, which consisted of five hours
of competition dancing by students of all schools
in the district, most youngsters, even those of five
or six years old, carried empty bottles which they
would occasionally swig, acting progressively more
inebriated throughout the dance. Those that most
realistically mimed their parents' drunkenness were
most applauded.

Soqa Catholics celebrate five religious fiestas
(aside from the four secular fiestas patrias, which
include speeches and parades and in which Adventists
also participate). These are Año Nuevo, Carnival (in

---

*Pusitunka is Aymara for "forty" and refers to the
fact that their crude, sugared alcohol, purchased in
gallon tin cans, is cuarenta grados or 40%. This
is equivilant to 80 proof. However, the alcohol is
much more raw than liquor sold in the U.S., and at
an altitude of over two miles it is far more potent
than similar spirits would be at sea level, as many
a gringo has learned to his distress.

February), Pentecost, Dia de Santiago, and Octavo de Santiago. The first four of these utilize personally-owned costumes and local flute-and-drum music. Pentecost, which in Church tradition celebrates the descent of the Holy Spirit on the apostles, has been assimilated by the Aymara as a harvest rite. Octavo de Santiago, dedicated to the god of lightning whose statue is kept in a small chapel on Soqa, supposedly lasts eight days, though in 1976 it lasted only four. This is by far the biggest fiesta of the year for Soqeños and the only one which is expensive: a brass band must be hired from the mainland and costumes must be rented. Each of Soqa's five dance groups chooses one of the fourteen or so stereotyped dances--the cullavada, llamarada, diablada, morinada, etc.--dancing in the morning at the house of the alferado and in the afternoon moving to an open area near the western end of the island where a great crowd gathers to watch. Since five brass bands are playing different music simultaneously, the cacaphony is tremendous.

The Buechlers (1971: 69-70) report a systematic cargo system in Campi, Bolivia, with a hierarchically ordered system of prestige offices. No such thing exists in any of the three communities of my study, and probably does not exist for most communities on the Peruvian side of the Titicaca Basin. Rather than an ordered series of offices, there is generally but one office, that of alferado, sometimes called cabeza (head). In towns, where great sums of money are spent, this can be a prestige position, and even in the campo it can be used to gain prestige if one wants to spend enough money. However, in many parts of the campo, where a myth

103

of equality exists, _alferados_ are not chosen according to ability to pay, but according to age, length of time since last being _alferado_, or on a rigid rotation basis. In the latter case, there is little status involved _per se_ in the position of _alferado_.

In the towns, where fiestas will almost always be financed by _mestizos_ or _cholos_, and where pressure is put upon the richest families--some of whom live most of the year in Ariquipa or Lima--fiesta costs may run to enormous sums. One _alferado_ in Huancané claimed to have spent $4,110, which included $457 for the virgin's dress, $228 for one band and $450 for a second band, and $913 for beer. Presumably the other $2,000 was spent for entertaining in his house, for new clothes, and to pay for a special mass and other Catholic rites.

In the _campo_, expenses are much less. _Alferados_ in Soqa are selected on a strict, no-refusal rotation basis, and, even then, one is responsible for but one day of any fiesta. Thus the average cost for the most expensive fiesta, _Octavo de Santiago_, was only $157, and the highest amount reported was $205. The average for the second costliest fiesta, Carnival, which does not require hiring a band, was $40. In addition, only 42% of Catholic families reported having been _alferado_ since 1971. A major reason for these low figures is that much of the costs will not be in money but in animals and produce already owned by the _alferado_. The following shows a breakdown of money costs, averaged from my two most complete reports, for one day of the _Octavo de Santiago_ fiesta:

Music	$51
Alcohol	10

Beer	$63
Rice	2
Noodles	1
Sugar	1
Bread	3
Vegetables	3
Fruit	1
Chickens	10
Eggs	1
Total	$146

With average family income $551 per year (much of which is spent on the coast), this is hardly sufficient to put anyone in debt for very long, even considering the alferado's own contribution of a pig, potatoes, oca, chuño, barley, and perhaps a new outfit for himself and his wife.

If we must look for a function for the fiesta system, we need not look very far beyond the patently obvious: fiestas offer momentary release from a dreary existence. Yet, as we have seen, fiestas used to be a strong factor in holding together loosely structured ayllus. Also, fiestas are sometimes viewed as redistributive systems, as means of gaining prestige and determing leadership, and as "leveling mechanisms" to maintain a relative equality of wealth. In ayllu times, possibly all of these functions were important; today none of them are. There is little redistribution, because what is spent is mainly money earned outside the community. Though one sometimes sees "prestige battles" with one alferado trying to outspend his predecessor of the year before, these competitions collapse in two or three years, so most spend within typical and expected parameters. The rotational system deprives the alferado of any implicit status and precludes any leveling function. Finally, most dance groups are

confined to aini groups or families occupying a
certain area, so fiestas tend to be more conducive
to segmentation than to the cohesion of the whole
community.

In towns, a new function is definitely formative.
More and more, the wealthier mestizos and cholos are
moving away from small towns or villages into the
cities, such as Puno, Ariquipa, or Lima. Yet they
retain land, often highly profitable land, near the
towns they have left. With intense population pressure on land, and with indigenous population increasingly believing that land belongs to those who
work it, it becomes essential that these absentee
owners retain their place of prominence within the
community. Sponsorship of a fiesta has become the
most important means to this end; a man who is alferado remains an integral part of the community,
although he may visit only once a year. A primary
function of the fiesta is thus the assertion of land
rights by absentee owners.

This function is rapidly entering the campo.
In Soqa, where 29% of those who work outside the
community have jobs in construction, factories, and
mining--jobs requiring a ten to twelve month contract
--and where many others work on the coast for more
than four months a year, the fiesta system may become
a means by which one can establish his continuing
place in the community and, more, his right to lands
deserted or worked by others for the larger part of
the year.

SUMMARY
A systems analysis of Aymara religious belief
and practices reveals several of the same processes

which we saw in relation to social structure: a
diminishing in importance of the more traditional
forms and an increase in the relevance of external
forms, a general opening-up of a previously relatively closed system, and a process by which inputs
and outputs mutually reinforce one another and thus
lead to a continual opening up of the system.

The indigenous religion is still central to the
Aymara, but there has been a tendency for it to be
reduced from a holistic system, encompassing both
belief and practice, to a largely ritual system,
devoted mainly to magical control in those areas
where there is little practical control. This process, which may have been going on for a long time,
was amplified by recent economic changes. Such
secular inputs into the religious subsystem as formal
education based on mestizo models, and values derived from wage labor on the coast, have increasingly
diminished the relevance of Aymara indigenous
theology. But new technological inputs--such as
modern medicine, lightning rods, or chemical ferti-
lizer--which would give campesinos control over
their environment, have not been forthcoming, with
the result that magical control remains the only
control in many areas of campo life.

If the traditional Aymara religious world view
is seen as one of the more rigid of boundaries encompassing the peasant system, then the breaching of
this boundary opens possibilities for new attitudes,
based on Christian or scientific concepts of the
world. Such concepts may be adaptive in the wider
world of wage labor and district government, just as
the indigenous religion was adaptive to the tight
world of subsistence agriculture. While I have no

107

direct evidence that campesinos are indeed becoming more Catholic, this might be a logical prediction given the partial vacuum created by the diminishment of traditional belief systems, by the increase in formal education taught by Catholic mestizos, and by the strong place that Catholicism holds in the world outside the Aymara community. What is already observable is that the fiesta system, which is the fullest (and sometimes only) expression of Aymara popular Christianity, has lost many of the functions it had only thirty or so years ago and is developing a primary new function, that of allowing absentee land owners to reassert their property rights.

We have yet to examine how these economic changes are affecting the Protestant minority. Here the effects are so profound, and so surprising, that the following chapter is devoted entirely to this subject.

7. The Adventist Elite

The Seventh Day Adventists are not the only
Protestant denomination represented in the Peruvian
altiplano, but they are by far the largest such
group. Eleven per cent of the respondents to
Hickman's (1963: 211) six-community questionnaire
claimed to be Adventists. Escobar (1967: 50, 67)
suggests there are more or less 10,000 Adventists in
the department of Puno, while the Adventists themselves claim twice that number.

The Seventh Day Adventists are fundamentalist
Protestants, distinguished from other fundamentalist
denominations by their insistence on Saturday as
their day of religious observation and rest. Missionization, which commenced at the end of the first
decade of this century, focused intensively on education, so today virtually all those born into this
religion can read their Castillian Spanish Bibles,
which they believe with the utmost literalness.
Unlike Adventism in the United States, there is little
need for a concerted attack against the theory of
evolution; such heresies are unheard of in the altiplano. Nor has the doctrine of the imminent end of
the world and the Second Coming of Christ assumed
the importance it has in the U.S.; one born Adventist

was surprised when I told him this was a major tenet
of Adventism in my country. Far more important than
doctrine is the Adventists' rigid abstinence from
alcohol, coca, and, for some, pork, though unlike
their U.S. counterparts, vegetarianism is not observed except of economic necessity. I have heard
numerous claims that Adventists do like to drink
liquor now and then, and sometimes actively participate in fiestas. This was not true of the family
with which I lived, and did not appear to be true of
regular church attenders. They consciously, and
sometimes vehemently, repudiate both the Catholic
and indigenous religions.

The Adventists of Soqa are largely second,
third, or fourth generation. Their church-school
complex is one of the largest building groups on the
island, rivaled only by the public school. They have
recently completed a costly new temple--much larger
than the earlier one which will now be made into a
classroom. Such projects are paid, not out of the
nominal church offerings, but through equal assess-
ments of labor and money for all member families.

The altiplano Seventh Day Adventist church is
totally native; foreign missionaries sometimes visit
but do not direct. The structure of the church is
hierarchical, though nowhere nears so rigidly as within
Catholicism. The Adventist center in Puno acts more
in an administrative than authoritative capacity.
At the district level is the pastor, the native
missionary of the area who officiates over several
community groups. Since a hundred members are
necessary to form a "church," most communities, including Soqa, have grupos, which will be locally
directed by an Anciano de la Iglesia (Elder of the

Church). This position is presently not filled on Soqa, so the lower-status _Jefe del Grupo_ assumes these functions. In addition, there is a Director of Missionary Activity and a Director of the Saturday School.

In Soqa, Saturday service takes place at the church on the hill and lasts supposedly from 9:30 a.m. to noon, and then from three to four p.m. Though there is considerable variation in this pattern, service seldom lasts less than three and a half or four hours. There are three parts to the service: the first, of about an hour and a half, is Saturday school, consisting of Bible lessons; the second service, the _Culta Divina_, is the church service proper; finally, after a communal lunch, is the service given by the _Sociedad Jovenes Missioneros Voluntarios_, a group of young people who have volunteered to proselytize on the mainland.

The actual service showed considerable variation from this pattern. One morning service I attended began at ten a.m. and lasted until 1:45 p.m. before lunch break. The church had benches on the left side for the men; the women, with their children, sat on the floor in the rear and along the right side. There were twenty-three men, around fifteen women, and numerous children. The service began with singing, and between speeches or during periods when no one seemed to know what to do, there was singing. All the men had hymnals in Spanish, and anyone could propose a song simply by calling out its number in the book. Singing was followed by announcements--such as school needs for books-- then a young women read the minutes of the last morning meeting. The second part opened with

singing, a prayer, and a short sermon. Several
different people officiated in these activities. The
short sermon was followed, after singing and prayer,
by a longer sermon, and this was followed by roll
call and collection, a few soles at the most being
the largest donation. After this, the director of
the Adventist school talked on church and school
needs; this was the only part of the service in
Spanish, except for singing and Bible readings,
because the school director is from the north of
the lake and speaks Quechua rather than Aymara. A
very long sermon, of almost an hour, given by the
district pastor, terminated the morning service.
Lunch on the ground in front of the school consisted
of oca, potatoes, and beans, each woman placing her
contribution upon a shawl until a large, colorful
pile had accumulated. Everyone helped himself.
There was a great deal of conversation, joking, and
laughter. After lunch, about two thirds of the group
straggled reluctantly back into church for the afternoon service. The morning service had gone well
overtime, and no one seemed enthusiastic. Songs
were alternated with brief Bible readings from a
pamphlet and discussions of the readings. After
an hour the service more faded away than formally
ended. Outside, the men gathered to discuss problems of the school and the construction of the new
church building.

Interested adults may also get together Wednesday morning, and from five to six Friday afternoon
to study the Bible and sing. For the Aymara, who
until this century were universally illiterate, the
educational import of these Bible study meetings
should not be underestimated. Wednesdays before

school and Saturdays before regular service, the
children have their own program, roughly equivalent
to the Sunday School of other denominations, consisting of religious songs, games, Bible readings, and
other activities.

Tensions between Catholic and Protestant on
Soqa are minimal but do exist. One of my Adventist
informants was afraid to go near a local fiesta
because so many Catholics, when drunk, threatened
to punch him in the nose. Such tension may arise
less from religious differences than from the fact
that the Adventists--as we shall see--are an elite.
As for the Adventist attitude toward Catholics, it
is more disdainful than hostile. "No pueden cali-
ficar," observed one Adventist informant, "They
simply don't count" (or, more literally, "They can't
qualify").

ADVENTISM: A STATISTICAL PORTRAIT

Protestants in largely Catholic societies have
been portrayed in anthropological literature as
marginals, as possessed of anomie and disillusion-
ment, as pawns of capitalistic imperialism. Carter
(1965b:389-91) found the fifteen per cent Adventists
in the Bolivian community of Irpa Chico to be
generally wealthier than their Catholic neighbors,
but "frustrated and disillusioned" from having
repudiated their own traditions, and in the process
of passing from prominence to marginality. Keesing
(1976: 461) concisely presents the anthropological
viewpoint:

> One of the many impediments to the success of
> fundamentalist Protestant missionaries has
> been the austerity and emptiness of the new
> life proferred in place of the old. A pall of

113

Protestant gloom hangs over many a community in the Pacific and tropical South America that once throbbed with life, laughter, and song.

...Protestantism, as Weber (1956) and Tawney (1926) have compellingly argued, has historically been closely associated with the rise of capitalism, supported indirectly by the corporate wealth of Europe and the United States.... Christianity has been a direct instrument of imperialism to spread religion while gaining raw materials, markets, and cheap labor.

The anthropologist, immersed in such professional stereotypes, might well expect to find the Adventists on Soqa to be a disillusioned group of anomic marginals joylessly repudiating their heritage while lusting shamelessly after Western goods.

The actual picture is somewhat different. Adventists, and one Jehovah's Witness (born Adventist), comprise forty-eight of Soqa's 261 families. This 18% minority:

...holds the bulk of political power. Four of the top six positions are held by the Adventists, and they also hold 37% of all non-religious positions (see Figure 5.1, page 80);

...has more, and considerably better, schooling than Catholics (4.47 years for Adventist men, 3.05 years for Catholic men);

...has larger families than Catholics (Adventist 5.22 persons, Catholic 4.43);

...has almost the same per capita income, but an 18% larger per family income (Adventist $633, Catholic $519. Figures are 1976 U.S. dollars, converted from soles);

...buys, fattens, and sells slightly more bulls

114

per year (Adventist 1.28, Catholic 1.22);

...includes significantly* more men in the
lucrative profession of musician (Adventist 15%
of household heads, Catholic 04%);

...includes a greater number of families that
sell in the Acora market (Adventist 13%,
Catholic 06%);

...includes a greater per cent of its circular
migrants who work in the longer-term, more
profitable jobs in construction, mining, and
factory work (Adventist 40% of work force,
Catholic 23%);

...takes out seventeen times as many loans from
the Banco Agropecuario to buy cattle to fatten
and sell (Adventists 17% of households, Catholics 01%).

...has more corrugated metal roofs (Adventist
1.54 roofs per family complex, Catholic 1.26);

...has more possessions (on a list of eleven
items, Adventists scored significantly higher on
six and slightly higher on three).

In regards to opinions, Adventists:

...showed significantly higher pro-education
scores on all four questions designed to measure this factor;

...showed one slightly higher score and two
significantly higher scores on questions designed to measure orientation to capitalism

---

*"Significance" in all cases is determined by the
chi square test at .05 significance level.

(note also the significant amount of loans taken out, showing the ability to plan ahead and take economic chances);

...chose education over profit on three questions which put these factors in conflict;

...and, surprisingly, showed themselves as more traditional on some questions designed to measure this factor.

In sum, we find on Soqa not a group of frustrated and disillusioned marginals, but a relatively educated, slightly traditional elite which holds political and economic power out of proportion to their meager numbers.

Why?

If we have saved this problem until last, it is because the answer depends on an understanding of the economic, governmental, and social changes that presently pervade Aymara culture.

THE WEBERIAN HYPOTHESIS

The relationship between Protestantism and capitalism has become a commonplace since Max Weber's classic The Protestant Ethic and the Spirit of Capitalism (1956, orig. 1904). It is, therefore, something of a kneejerk response to hypothesize that this relation is the key to understanding the exceptional wealth, education, and political power of Soqa's Adventists. The problem is to search out that area where capitalism is most related to religion.

Actually, "capitalism" can mean many things. Generally, it implies entrepreneurial activities. However, such enterprises are lacking in Soqa; there

116

Table 7.1
SOQA ADVENTIST/CATHOLIC COMPARISONS[a]
ECONOMY

	Advent- ist	Cath- olic	Soqa Total
Per capita income (U.S. $)[b]	$116	$117	$117
Per family income	$633	$519	$551
Money entering community per family (does not include money spent on the coast)[c]	$406	$279	$314
Sell in market	.13	.06	.08
Musicians	.15	.04	.07
Average number of bulls fattened and sold per year per family	1.28	1.22	1.24
Number household heads who work outside Soqa	.70	.75	.74
Types of work: fraction of work force			
chacras	.53	.70	.74
construction	.27	.16	.21
factories, mining	.20	.07	.10
Types of work: months per year worked by average worker			
chacras	3.6	4.0	3.9
construction	9.3	5.2	6.5
factories, mining	10.3	12.0	10.8

[a]For sizes of samples see Appendix A.

[b]Lower Adventist income reflects larger families.

[c]Large difference reflects greater number of Adventists in mining and construction jobs. Those working chacras spend almost all their pay on the coast.

Table 7.2

SOQA ADVENTIST/CATHOLIC COMPARISONS
ORIENTATION TO CAPITALISM

	Advent-ist	Cath-olic	Soqa Total
Per cent of families which have taken loans from the Banco Agropecuario to purchase and fatten cattle	.17	.01	.06
Questionnaire questions			
D. In your opinion the principal objective of raising cattle is:			
1. To demonstrate to everyone the wealth of the owner.	.00	.01	.01
2. For food and wool.	.68	.81	.77
3. To sell in order to earn money.*	.32	.19	.22
4. In order to earn money, it is a good idea to take a loan from the Banco Agropecuario.*			
Agree	.29	.04	.09
Disagree	.68	.95	.89

*Significant difference as determined by chi square test at .05 significance level.

Table 7.3

SOQA ADVENTIST/CATHOLIC COMPARISONS
POSSESSIONS

	Advent-ist	Cath-olic	Soqa Total
Number calamina roofs per family	1.54	1.26	1.34
Fraction of families having the following articles			
*Bed	.74	.56	.62
Pressure kerosene stove	.98	.92	.95
*Table	.46	.20	.26
*Chairs	.30	.12	.17
Sewing machine	.52	.44	.46
*Flashlight	.15	.03	.07
*Pressure lantern	.20	.03	.06
Radio	.67	.76	.74
*Latrine	.07	.01	.02
Bicycle	.35	.26	.29
Motorcycle	.02	.03	.03

*Significant difference as determined by chi square test at .05 significance level.

Table 7.4

SOQA ADVENTIST/CATHOLIC COMPARISONS
AVERAGE ADULT SCHOOLING

	Advent-ist	Cath-olic	Soqa Total
Schooling in years (reported scores probably slightly inflated for all groups)			
Men	4.47	3.05	3.45
Women	2.02	1.41	1.58
Men and women	3.20	2.19	2.47

Table 7.5

SOQA ADVENTIST/CATHOLIC COMPARISONS
ATTITUDE TOWARD EDUCATION

	Advent-ist	Cath-olic	Soqa Total
A. What is the most important objective in life?			
1. To earn a lot of money.	.29	.42	.38
*2. To give one's children a good education.	.34	.11	.17
3. To enjoy life.	.37	.48	.45
4. To earn the respect of the community.	.00	.00	.00
B. If you had at this time 10,000 soles to spend as you wish, how would you spend it?			
1. Give a fiesta.	.04	.01	.01
2. Feed the family.	.39	.77	.67
3. Buy cattle to fatten and sell.	.32	.16	.20
*4. Educate your children.	.20	.03	.08
5. Invest in a business, such as a shop.	.07	.00	.02
E. The best inheritance for one's children is:			
*1. Education.	.20	.02	.06
2. Land.	.80	.96	.92
3. Money.	.00	.02	.01
10. By means of education, one can make of oneself that which one wants.			
*Agree	.71	.44	.51
Disagree	.27	.55	.47

*Adventists significantly higher as measured by the chi square test at .05 significance level.

Table 7.6
SOQA ADVENTIST/CATHOLIC COMPARISON
TRADITIONALISM

	Advent-ist	Cath-olic	Soqa Total
8. Machines make men lazy.			
*Agree	.20	.05	.09
Disagree	.80	.95	.91
9. Coca and cards tell the truth.			
Agree	.02	.13	.10
*Disagree	.98	.80	.94
13. A family of only girls is cursed.			
*Agree	.15	.03	.06
Disagree	.83	.97	.94
15. The birth of twins signifies a punishment of god.			
Agree	.02	.16	.12
*Disagree	.98	.86	.88
17. It is better never to pay money to buy food.			
Agree	.04	.08	.08
Disagree	.96	.84	.92
20. To have a better life, we must return to the traditional life of our ancestors.			
Agree	.04	.02	.02
Disagree	.96	.97	.97

*Adventists show significantly higher score as measured by the chi square test at .05 significance level.

121

are no shops or small-scale industries, and marketing of produce is minimal. The fattening of cattle might be called "entrepreneurial," but this is a firmly grounded institution among the Aymara to the extent that almost all families practice it, and the difference in number of bulls sold is not significant between Catholics and Adventists. Nor is the "free market" a useful criterion of capitalism in our case, as this is obviously the same for everyone in the area.

Clearly, if we are to test some sort of Weberian hypothesis, we will need a definition of "capitalism" more in line with the actual situation on Soqa. We might best define the term narrowly, focusing on the concept of capital, as <u>the tendency to invest surplus capital back into the means of production</u>. Here we have a definition we can use, because apparently the fiesta system drains Catholic capital in a nonproductive manner, while Protestants are able to utilize their wealth productively.

We can now state our hypothesis: <u>People with a more capitalistic orientation, who want to escape the costs of the fiesta system in order to more productively invest their money, are attracted to Adventism, thus forming an economic elite.</u>

Such a hypothesis poses something of a chicken-or-egg problem: did the orientation to capitalism come first, or did the Adventism create the orientation to capitalism? We can escape this by formulating a feedback process, by which Adventism and capitalism are mutually reinforcing.

However, no matter how we state it, the hypothesis is patently false.

In order to validate the hypothesis, it would

be necessary to show (1) that the fiesta system
actually does drain significant amounts of capital
from the community; (2) that the Adventists invest
significantly more in money-making activities; and
(3) that the financial motive is a strong one for
people converting to Adventism. All of these were
tested; none of them are true.

First, the fiesta system simply does not cost
that much. There is no cargo system, no hierarchy
of offices, and alferados are appointed on a rigid,
no-refusal rotation basis, so no one is ever chosen
as sponsor of a major fiesta more than once every
five to eight years. Since one serves but one day
of a major fiesta, costs for 1975 to mid-1976 aver-
aged only $157 for the biggest fiesta (Octavo de
Santiago), $40 for the second largest (Carnival),
and a mere $23 for the third largest (Santiago).

These figures do not include non-money costs,
such as agricultural produce and perhaps a pig or
sheep, but as these are seldom sold in any case, they
would not form money capital. As the family income
of Soqa Catholics is $519 per year, of which $279
enters the community, it is obvious that the fiesta

Table 7.7

REPORTED* FIESTA COSTS, SOQA, 1975 TO MID-1976

	Octavo de Santiago	Carnival		Pentacost	Santiago
	$126	$43	$34	None reported	$23
	137	34	34	for this per-	23
	205	46	46	iod	—
	160	46	—		
Average	$157	$40			$23

*Many did not respond to this question

123

system, as practiced in Soqa, is not tying up a
great deal of available capital.

Nor are the Adventists investing much more than
the Catholics. Virtually the only money investment
in production is in buying cattle to fatten and
sell. While the Adventists do buy more cattle, and
are willing to take out loans to do so, the difference, 1.28 to 1.22 bulls per year, is not significant. Most of the difference between Adventist and
Catholic incomes is due to the fact that Adventists
work the more lucrative jobs on the coast, and that
more of them play in bands--professions that require
very little capital investment.

Of the five new Adventists interviewed as to
their motives for converting, only one seemed to have
an economic motive: he was from a poor family and
"married up" to a wealthier Adventist girl, accepting
conversion as part of the marriage deal. Carter's
(1965b: 386) life history interviews with thirty-nine
urban Protestants in Tacna revealed a finanical
motive for only one. In addition, as we have seen,
Adventists on Soqa strongly and consistently chose
education over wealth on my questionnaire whenever
the two were put in conflict.

A closer look at the statistics on the Adventists and Catholics of Soqa reveals that differences
in wealth and investment are real, but relatively
small. The truly large difference, one measured
both in average attained grade levels and in attitudes, is in the area of education. It is here
that we must seek our alternative hypothesis.

THE EDUCATION-AS-SELECTIVE-FACTOR HYPOTHESIS

The large majority of Soqa Adventists were born
Adventists, generally of the third or fourth generation. If we assume that people will normally remain
in the religion in which they were born, and will
accept the values passed on to them by their families, then we must ask: What were the crucial factors
in the establishment of the Adventist church on
Soqa? Such a question can be tied to our concern
with education if we hypothesize: The active selective factor in the formation of the Adventist church
on Soqa was not money but education. Adventism
offered educational opportunities not available
elsewhere, and thus attracted a group of people more
progressive, independent, and intellectual than the
norm. These values were reinforced by the teachings
of the new denomination, and have been passed on for
several generations.

This is something of a Darwinian hypothesis,
which must be tested historically. Fortunately, we
have a very complete history of the founding of the
Adventist church in the altiplano in the writings of
F. A. Stahl (1920) and J. B. A. Kessler, Jr. (1967).
The history of Adventism on Soqa was well known by
my informants.

The story begins at the turn of the century with
a young man named Manuel Zuñiga Camacho, who was
sent by his family from his home in Plateria to work
the nitrate mines in Chile. There he attended a
Protestant school and, while remaining unconverted,
became convinced that education was the answer to
his people's oppression and poverty. Returning to
Plateria, he started the altiplano's first campesino
school, in 1904, and immediately came into conflict

125

with the Church, at that time one of the strongest forces in Peru for the maintenance of the status quo. One priest argued in a sermon that "God never intended them to go to school and get learning. Their business was to attend to their sheep and crops and if they persisted in attending school their crops would be blighted and disease would kill their flocks" (John Ritchie, quoted in Kessler 1967: 228-29). Zuñiga led a delegation to Lima to ask the president of the republic for schooling and protection from injustices, but the trip was unsuccessful and pressure from the Church, especially the bishop in Puno, caused the closing of the incipient school in 1907.

It was at this time that Zuñiga made contact with the Adventists. Hoping the presence of foreigners might restrain the constant persecution, he went to Ariquipa to ask the Adventist mission there to support his school. Though his trip was motivated by desire for education, not religion, he converted to Adventism while in Ariquipa, possibly as a condition of Adventist support.

In 1908 it was arranged that Frederick and Ana Stahl, recently appointed to Bolivia, would devote half their time to helping Zuñiga. Today Stahl is all but worshipped by altiplano Adventists; I don't know how many times I have heard campesinos say with great pride, "Fernando* Stahl, himself, taught in our school," or "Fernando Stahl visited here in 1911." The reverence is justified. Stahl's book, En el pais de los Incas, reveals a sharp and

---

*I have never learned why campesinos always refer to Frederick as Fernando.

126

surprisingly open and compassionate mind, great
courage, and dedication without fanaticism. He is
open about the mistakes of his first years, when he
bumbled about the altiplano selling tracts and
pamphlets to campesinos who could not read, getting
run out of various towns by priests who insisted
he was the Devil. It is clear that even when the
Plateria school reopened in 1909 under Adventist
auspices, it was Zuñiga's and not Stahl's operation.
However, by 1911, when Stahl was assigned full time
to Plateria, the blundering novice missionary had
become a sophisticated professional. He had seen
that campesinos were attracted to the tiny mission
in Plateria not because of the beauties of attending
church on Saturday, but because of the school and
inchoate clinic. In essence, he had learned to sell
a package deal, and this resulted in one of the
greatest Adventist successes in all of South America.

The package deal consisted of education, health,
and religion, roughly in that order. The school
was already established, though the building, along
with the mission and dispensary, were not constructed until 1913. Ana Stahl was the dispensary
nurse, and in 1914 took over the school also.
School was taught in Spanish, with good reason: the
primary function was to allow campesinos to read the
Bible, and Bibles were written in Spanish. This had
important ramifications for the future.

In 1911, Frederick Stahl visited Soqa, invited
by Pedro Cutipa, grandfather of the present president of Soqa, and at that time cacique or headman
of the island community. The majority of the people
had little interest in the new religion and perhaps
perceived that education had no relevance to their

closed world of subsistence agriculture. Nevertheless, Pedro accepted Stahl's invitation to come to
the school in Plateria. Pedro later returned to
Soqa and began to teach the reading and writing he
had learned, without trying to make converts. It
was only when Stahl visited again in 1914 that the
Soqa Adventist church was founded secretly. Stahl
returned to teach in 1916. By this time there were
about five families professing Adventism and conduct-
ing secret services and schooling in Pedro Cutipa's
house. They were, of course, the only people on
Soqa who were literate, just as the Adventists, in
general, were the only campesinos in the entire altiplano who could read and write. They were also
some of the very few campesinos who could speak
Spanish.

Meanwhile, persecution began to intensify.
Education was a severe threat to the mestizos,
who systematically exploited the Indians through
forced labor service, arbitrary taxes of produce and
animals, and systematic land theft for which the
ignorant peasant had no legal defense. The priests,
whose power was based on the continuing ignorance
and subservience of the campesino, were especially
threatened. On March 3, 1913, Valentin Ampuero,
Bishop of Puno, retaliated with force; with two
hundred Indians recruited from Chucuito, he marched
to Plateria, broke into the newly completed mission,
ransacked the various buildings, and had the six
occupants beaten, tied up, and dragged off to jail
in Puno when they refused to kiss his hand. Stahl
and his wife were missionizing in the campo at the
time, but among the prisoners was Zuñiga.

Though the group was eventually released,

128

persecution continued. Adventists were beaten at
random. Stahl (1920: 70) accuses a priest of beating
a convert to death with a cudgel. Since Adventists
were not permitted to drink alcohol by their religion, a common harrassment, especially during
fiestas, was to hunt them down and pour pusitunka
down their throats until they were drunk. When the
Stahls set to work building the small hospital in
the mission complex in Plateria, a priest threatened
to have anyone who helped arrested. Death threats
were common.

All of this was more or less legal, since there
was, at the time, a constitutional law to the effect
that Catholicism was the state religion and anyone
directing religious services other than Catholic
could be incarcerated up to three years. I have
been told by campesino informants that there were
also department or district laws forbidding the edu-
cating of Indians. However, partially because of
the publicity surrounding the March 3 arrests, plus
the support of a Puno newspaper which favored
Adventist missionization because of its beneficial
effects on the campesinos, the law restricting
religion was removed from the constitution in
November of 1915.

This did not stop persecution, which in the
Quechua region to the north of the lake was even
more ferocious than among the Aymara, perhaps
because in that area large-scale landowners,
hacendados, were being threatened. Adventist
converts were imprisoned up to five years. The
first school, built in 1920, was razed to the ground.
Later, two hundred Catholic Indians attacked the
school at Laro, but were driven off by twice their

129

number of defenders. In another incident twelve
Adventists were killed in a single afternoon. Later,
fifteen were killed.

On Soqa the Adventists had come out in the
open. The Adventist school was formally begun in
1916 with about twenty students in Pedro Cutipa's
house. In 1921, Pedro himself went to Lima and
successfully secured authorization for the school
from the Ministry of Education. Legal recognition
opened the way for the construction of the first
school building, which was attended by perhaps
thirty students. This school remained in existence,
also serving as Adventist church, until 1952. Persecution, including physical abuse, continued on
Soqa despite legal recognition. Pedro Cutipa was
paying for his dedication to education and his new
religion; he had passed from community leader,
respected cacique, to the ostracized leader of a
persecuted minority

By 1920, the Stahls, who had spent twelve years
at 12,500 feet, had to return to the United States
for reasons of health. Their work was carried on
by E. H. Wilcox, who set a matriculation fee of two
soles a year (75¢) and required that to attain
Adventist educational support applicants must
furnish a completely equipped school building and
assure a student body of at least eighty students.
Despite such restrictions, schools were an idea
whose time had come. In 1922 an Adventist teachers-
training college was established in Juliaca to supply
teachers for the burgeoning Adventist school system,
which had grown by 1924 to eighty community schools
with an enrollment of 4,150. Two years later there
were two hundred community schools. These Adventist

schools, it should be noted, still provided the only
educational opportunities available to campesinos.

Perhaps stimulated by a growth of consciousness
arising from education, the conflict between mestizos
and campesinos increased in intensity toward the end
of the twenties. Pedro Cutipa went again to Lima,
this time to beseech the Leguía government to
give equal liberty to Adventists and Catholics.
Leguía responded in 1929 by passing a law against
teaching any religion but Catholicism in schools, a law
which had no effect, so well established were Adventist schools by this time. Nevertheless, other legislation favorable to campesinos was passed.

A Depression cutback in missionary personnel
and support resulted in a decline in the number of
schools during the thirties, to eighty in 1937.
That year saw the first of the state-supported
schools in the altiplano but on such a small scale
that it was not until ten years later that the nation
really got into the school business in this area.
The public school of Soqa was not established until
1952. It took some time for competition with
Adventist schools to be felt; as late as 1950 there
were still 166 Adventist schools in the altiplano.
However, ten years later, competition from free
public schools had reduced that number to 47. In
the mid-seventies, Adventist schooling seemed to be
undergoing a resurgence, as the higher quality of
Adventist teaching became a known fact; over half
the students in the Adventist school of Soqa come
from Catholic families despite the $32 per student
tuition.

It should be obvious that the history of formal
education on the Peruvian altiplano is largely a

history of Adventistm. On Soqa, Adventists had a
thirty-six-year head start in education over the
Catholics, and since the first students were adults,
these decades reach to the third generation. A
three-generation advance in literacy and in values
associated with education could not help but have
the most profound social ramifications for both
Adventist and Catholic.

Looking again at the founding of the Adventist
church in the altiplano, we can see that converts
were being asked to give up much, to endure more.
They had to repudiate some of their traditions, their
fiestas, their alcohol and coca, sometimes their kin
ties. They became persecuted outcasts, ostracized,
beaten, sometimes killed. And for what?

It is difficult to believe that they repudiated
all this, endured all this, for the sake of cele-
brating the sabbath on Saturday rather than Sunday.
But that they would do it for education is believable; for a select few, ignorance is a small death,
education a coming alive. In addition, many may have
been aware that education was the campesino's only
weapon against oppression.

I say "for a select few" because in the early
days they were a tiny minority. Adventism both
tapped and created a "pool of variability." It
served to select out of the mass of oppressed and
ignorant humans that meager group of deviants to
whom education had an almost addictive appeal, a
group who were not satisfied to be slaves to their
mestizo oppressors or to their own ignorance.
Manuel Zuñiga and Pedro Cutipa are examples of the
type of man upon whom this selective factor oper-
ated--highly intelligent leaders willing to

132

challenge the status quo.

It is facile to suggest that all significant
changes come about through invisible forces that
move entire groups of faceless people, as in some
Tolstoyan or Whitean panorama. Here we have not
masses but individuals--specific people with names
and personalities--preparing for an unforseeable
future fifty years before it arrives.

Support for the education hypothesis does not
only come from history. Statistics on the greater
schooling of the Adventists, by more than a full
grade, actually underestimate Adventist education,
since a single year of Adventist school might be
worth twice that of a public school. Public school
teachers are largely mestizos who, by law, have to
put in two years in the campo before they can get
jobs in the cities. Most of them do not speak
Aymara, and are isolated in the communities where
they are assigned. In such circumstances, they
sometimes work as little as possible. The
patronatos escolares, who are supposed to supervise
the school, are intimidated by the fact that education is free and is a function of the national
government, so there is little real supervision.
The situation is quite different for the Adventist
school. Since the school is totally run and financed
by the local Adventists, and by those Catholics
whose children go there, the patronatos escolares
are in a position to exercise their power, and
exercise it they do. Two or three times a week
they visit the school, sit in on classes, and confer
with teachers. School problems are brought up in
a scheduled period at church each Saturday. Exactly

133

contrary to public school practice, fiestas are few
and teachers are never absent without an excuse of
sickness or an official teachers meeting. Teachers
are all Adventists, and they can be discharged if
they do not fulfill their duties.

As one might expect, Adventists placed a
significantly higher value on education on every
question on the questionnaire designed to measure
this factor (Table 7.5). In the three questions
placing education in conflict with wealth (A, B, and
E), Adventists chose education significantly more
often than did Catholics.

These facts belie the implicit cynicism in
theories that hold that maximization focuses largely
or always on economic factors. When the Adventist
church started on Soqa back in 1914, education had
virtually no economic potential for the campesino.
Even while living very close to hunger, a small
group of campesinos was willing to devote a great
deal of time to a pursuit that was not related to
economic matters. Perhaps for the majority, the
stomach will be the locus of motivation, but for a
few, and these few often have influence far beyond
their numbers, education can be a primary driving
force.

THE MOTIVATION OF CONVERTS TODAY

Since education is today universally available,
and even the superior Adventist education is available to Catholics willing to pay tuition, the educational motive can no longer be sufficient cause
for conversion to Adventism. Interviews with five
converts, four in Soqa and one in Qollu K'uchu,
revealed the following motives: (1) sent to the coast

134

at age sixteen, the convert was given moral support, which he desperately needed, by Protestant missionaries; (2) one convert changed his religion to suit his Adventist mother after his Catholic father died; (3) one, already mentioned, "married up" to a wealthier Adventist woman; (4) one became converted as a result of a combination of factors, including marriage to an Adventist woman, education in an Adventist school, and disgust with the drunkenness associated with the Catholic fiesta system; (5) the last apparently converted while working on the coast as a cure for his own drunkenness.

Carter (1965b: 386), in his extensive study of Protestantism among Aymara workers on the coast, categorized the motives of thirty-five converts interviewed as: social isolation or break from the family (19 converts), sexual misbehavior or guilt (5), disappointment with Catholic clergy (4), divine healing (4), resentment of abusive confessionals (3), Protestant schooling (3), and financial difficulty (1).

To account for such diversity, we might follow Devereaux (1961) in distinguishing between personal motives and institutional motives. Here we can see that one institutional motive, desire for a better religion, acts as a funnel into which can be poured any number of varied personal motives. It should be noted, however, that economic motives are poorly represented, at either the personal or institutional level.

FROM MARGINAL TO ELITE

The crucial question remains: Why have the Adventists, who have been persecuted marginals for decades, become the leaders of the community?

The answer should be fairly obvious by now. If Adventist educational opportunities siphoned out of the mass of peasants a few who were deviant in the sense of being willing to suffer persecution in order to challenge the status quo, the original deviance of these people was hugely increased by adoption of the new religion. In repudiating the fiesta system, learning to speak Spanish, and becoming literate, these people became the most valuable part of that pool of variability which biologists recognize as essential to the processes of evolution.

For four decades the Adventists on Soqa remained both disruptive and dysfunctional. Their newly learned skills and values had no use since there was very little interaction with the Spanish-speaking world and the Aymara system remained tightly closed. On the contrary, their new beliefs created conflict and division within society and frustration and isolation for the Adventists themselves.

In 1952 all this changed. As we have seen, the breakdown of the ayllu system and its replacement with a modern corporate governmental structure was the first major response to the dimishment of the land base per family. Overnight, the conditions were set up by which the skills and values of the Adventists became not merely useful but essential. This pool of variability was better--far better-- adapted to the new conditions than was the Catholic majority. The new governmental structure meant open lines of communication to district and department agencies, increased contact with mestizos, and a growing involvement with legal paperwork. It is notable that the first major governmental input into

Soqa, the public school, coincided with the change in local governmental structure.

The Adventists were prepared; the Catholics were not. Few Catholics could speak Spanish, let alone read or write it, and Catholics had experienced only the most minimal and subservient dealings with mestizos. For forty years the Adventists had been reading, writing, and speaking Spanish, and had been involved in confronting the government and negotiating their rights as far as Lima.

Little wonder, then, that the Adventists stepped immediately into positions of leadership. They hold power today. The outline of the structure of Soqa government on page 80 shows how strongly that authority is entrenched. Four out of six top positions are held by Adventists, including that of president, and the man who holds this position is the guiding force in the community's ambitions to become a villa. Despite universal education today, Adventist influence is not diminishing but increasing. As Soqa continues its progression from subsistence agriculture to the money economy and from a closed society to an open society, the skills of reading, writing, counting, and, equally important, being able to assume at will certain mestizo attitudes and values, will become more and more important for the community. The status and power of the Protestant elite, who have a thirty-six-year head start in the skills that Catholics are only now learning, will increase accordingly.

ADVENTISTS AS "TRADITIONAL PROGRESSIVES"

A paradox emerges: Adventists do not seem to be any more progressive than the Catholics (see Table

7.6). In fact, for the two questions for which
Hickman (1963: 168) found the highest factor analysis relation to traditionalism, Soqa Adventists
scored significantly more traditional than Catholics.
Twenty per cent of Adventists and only 5% of Catholics agreed that "Machines make men lazy," and
15% of Adventists and 3% of Catholics agreed that
"A family that has only girls is cursed." The
overall picture is more ambiguous, with no significant difference on two questions, and Catholics
scoring more traditional on two. However, our
other data, which has shown Adventists to be more
in tune with modern trends, would imply the progressiveness which we simply do not find.

In addition, a popular conception, which has
seeped into scholarly works, is that Adventists
have a greater mobility toward becoming cholos or
mestizos (Escobar 1967: 67), a belief almost universally held among Catholic missionaries on the
altiplano. Carter (1965b) implies the same with his
theory that rural Protestants are essentially embrac-
ing Western culture and its wealth fetishism.

My data leads to opposite conclusions, more in
line with the CISEPA study (1967: 170) which found
that Adventists revealed higher norms and values in
relation to interpersonal confidence and cooperation
in the community. Escobar (1967: 243), despite his
views on the cholo-fication of Adventists, observes
that where they have become a majority, "one notes
a notable spirit of community...."

Obviously, the founders of the Adventist church
had to be more progressive, relative to the times,
than the Catholics. They were, by definition,
innovators. Once the struggle was fought, and won,

138

their grandsons and granddaughters could relax and settle back into the culture which their parents had once repudiated. The Adventist church, at least as manifested on Soqa, is now a fixed and accepted part of the community. The Adventists, being an elite, have, if anything, a stronger stake in that culture than do the Catholics. The Protestant church has become fixed, routinized, to the extent that adventurous Adventists are now converting to other religions: the island's only Jehovah's Witness was born an Adventist, and the altiplano's most prestigious Aymara priest, second only to the bishop in Juli, was a Soqa-born Adventist. The frontier mentality of those who struggled and fought to found the Adventist movement has given way in only a few generations to a conservative affirmation of the society, a situation very similar to that of immigrants in the United States.

If we are to find the anomic victims of rabid Protestant missionization--as the anthropological cliché would have it--we must look elsewhere than the Peruvian altiplano.

SUMMARY

William Carter (1965b: 389-91) was amazed to find that the small minority of Adventists in Irpa Chico, Bolivia, had more land, more latrines, more sheep, and more bicycles than Catholics, and participated to a surprising extent in local politics. Since his studies on the coast had been in complete agreement with conventional anthropological opinion that Protestants are poor, alienated marginals in Catholic countries, this discovery was absolutely contrary to expectation. The only explanation

available at the time was the Weberian explanation:
Protestants were those more inclined to adopt Western capitalistic values and pursue Western goods.
If this was the case, he reasoned, then these
Protestants must be "frustrated and disillusioned,"
having placed themselves beyond the pale of their
culture, and must, in effect, be on the way out.

I have never visited Irpa Chico, but I would
unhesitantly make the following prediction, which,
hopefully, may some day be checked: the Adventists
in Irpa Chico, thirteen years after Carter's study,
are thriving.

As we have seen, the Weberian hypothesis, as
applied to Aymara campesinos, must be flatly rejected. The promises of education and, to a lesser
extent, improved health, have filtered out of the
campesino masses a deviant group which created the
pool of variability adapted to economic conditions
today. These educated, Spanish-speaking deviants
are rapidly becoming the norm; it is they who have
set the pattern for the new steady state that will
be accomplished when the economic transformation
now in progress is complete.

8. Toward a New Stability

In systems terminology, the Aymara socio-
economic system, after four hundred years of morphostasis, is presently experiencing morphogenesis. It
is undergoing a fundamental transformation that
means a redefinition of the system's once rigid
and confining boundaries. Whereas negative feedback mechanisms kept the traditional system in a
"steady state," providing only the most minor ad-
justments possible to counter any inputs that had
seeped through the tight sieve of the boundaries,
now positive feedback is the order of the day.
The breakdown of subsistence agriculture as a way
of life resulted in such a severe breach in the
traditional boundaries that change has already been
manifested in virtually every major sector of the
system. We have already examined changes in the
economy, social structure, government, and
religion. Before proceeding to predict where the
system is heading, we need to examine a few more
areas of change, in language, in the degree of
"closedness" of the system, and in population.

THE AYMARA LANGUAGE

Along with the economy and community government, language has shown the greatest amount of
change within the last few decades. For centuries,
even after Spanish domination, the Aymara campesino
remained monolingual. Today, though Aymara is
universally spoken in the campo, virtually all men,
with the exception of the aged, are bilingual.
Aymara Spanish is not exactly that of Madrid; they
use only compound future and past tenses (always
preferring voy a ir to iré and he ido to fui, for
example) and seldom use any subjunctive form.
There is a tendency to terminate every phrase with
pue (a shortening of the Spanish pues, "well") or
no ma (a truncated form of no más, "no more"), and
in addition many speak Spanish with such a gutteral
accent that only other Aymara can understand them.
Nevertheless, Spanish is becoming sufficiently
prevalent that the Aymara language is already laden
with Spanish terms and idioms.

Ability in Spanish has a direct relationship
with one's job. Those who work only the rice
chacras need little bilingual ability, while a good
command of Spanish would be essential even to secure
a job in a mine or factory.

Since I employed community leaders to give
my questionnaire, I got to know such leaders well in
three widely divergent communities. All of these
spoke excellent Spanish. Such ability is undoubtedly
one of the essential qualities of leadership today,
since presidentes, tenientes, secretarios, and
various auxiliares must constantly deal with district
and department officials. This has diminished the

142

authority of the elders, who in _ayllu_ days were sought-after leaders, but who today do not have the linguistic qualifications for government.

With education at least through the primary grades universally available, Spanish ability and usage cannot but continue to increase at a rapid rate. Most altiplano teachers are _mestizos_ or are bilingual in Spanish and Quechua, so classes are almost never taught in any language except Spanish. In addition, all school textbooks are in Spanish. While Aymara will probably remain "the language of the soul," as I have heard it described, in a generation or so all Aymara men will be relatively proficient in their second language.

Even today adult women speak little more than the most rudimentary Spanish. They simply do not need it, since they seldom leave their communities except to go to market where almost all negotiations can be carried on in Aymara. This reinforces the woman's role as the strongest conservative force in the community, a role that is not likely to change in the immediate future since there are few opportunities for women outside the community. Women do not work on the coast; they seldom hold political positions; they have little contact with the outside world. Schools may teach women Spanish, but unless there is reinforcement outside the classroom, female bilingualism will remain nominal. Thus there is little evidence at this time that the woman's closed world of home, family, and _chacra_ is opening very rapidly.

143

THE CLOSED SYSTEM

Hewett wrote of the Aymara as he saw them around 1938: "The State finds it best to leave them alone. Here is a rare opportunity for the ethnologist who is seeking a tough job. Very rarely is a white man allowed to stay overnight in one of their villages" (quoted in LaBarre 1948: 39).

This is hardly the case today. I stayed many, many nights in a very remote community over a period of eight months, without any notable opposition. Two anthropologist friends, Paul and Winnie Brown, were not only invited to stay in a community by democratic decision of the whole group, but were given, rent free, a house to stay in. This is not to say that the Aymara have lost their suspicion of outsiders, but contact with outsiders has become so routine that they are no longer perceived as the threat they once were.

The barriers that for centuries enclosed the Aymara within a tight little world have been breached from both sides: the Aymara are going out; the mestizo culture and Western technology are coming in.

The traditional boundaries that kept the Aymara within their own culture were both internally and externally generated. Without, there was mestizo hostility and prejudice, and, more tangibly, constant attempts by mestizos to encroach on Aymara lands, usually through complex legal maneuvers against which the campesino was ill-equipped to defend himself. Prejudices continue, but the demand for a cheap labor supply on the coast has given the Aymara a crucial economic role in national development. The economic revolution in Bolivia, and its

144

brief counterpart under Velasco in Peru, provided
at least the rhetoric for a certain amount of
"consciousness raising" among campesinos, to the
extent that they are no longer reflexively subservient or tolerant of injustices to themselves. The
appropriations of hacienda land under Velasco removed
the threat of large-scale mestizo encroachment,
though replacing it with the threat, more imagined
than real, that privately held chacras would be
collectivized. Mestizos have become less of a
threat and the government has become more of a
presence in the campo, through SINAMOS, schools,
and the recent government takeover from the missionaries of the health promoter program. Technology, though available as early as the turn of the
century, has only significantly entered the campo
with the transition to the money economy, and today
finds its expression in kerosene stoves, radios,
sewing machines, and bicycles.

Traditional boundaries were as much imposed
from within as from without. The people did not
leave because they did not have to; the indigenous
culture supplied all needs, and in a comfortable and
secure context. The diminishment of the land base
beyond subsistence needs has changed all that. It
is now normal to leave the community for extended
periods, and confining ayllus have given way to local
governmental structures that provide efficient means
of transmitting requests to district officials.

The rigid boundaries that have so long enclosed
the Aymara have crumbled or are in the process of
doing so, giving way to boundaries much more flexible
and much less restrictive in regard to what is
permitted to enter or leave the campo.

POPULATION

All of the previously discussed effects of
economic changes are already discernable. A further
effect is not presently evident but is virtually
inevitable: rapid population growth.

Altiplano population growth remains slightly
less than that for Peru as a whole: Carter (1965b:
20) estimated 1.4 to 2.0 per cent per year for the
Bolivian side, while Peru's national rate at that
time was 2.8 per cent, rising to 3.3 per cent in
1972. The relatively low rate in the altiplano
is due to the extremely high child mortality
rate, 30% for the first five years in the three
communities studied. Seventy-seven per cent of
these die within the first year. This coincides
closely with Tschopik's (1951: 163) figures for
Chinchera in the early forties, which means that the
situation has not changed appreciably in about
thirty-five years

This is understandable. The only prophylactic
measure that has been introduced on a wide scale is
vaccination, but there are no preventative injections
for the real baby killers of malnutrition, pneumonia,
dysentery, and the ignorance of campesina midwives
who can only handle completely normal births.
Town clinics are looked upon as places to go to die,
obviously a self-fulfilling prophecy if no one goes
until they are past hope (even then, they are often
perceived as places to obtain legal death certifi-
cates, not for healing). Soqa never saw a nurse or
health promoter until mid-1976.

This situation cannot continue. Modern medicine
will come to the campo. Two factors have prevented

146

this in the past: first, the people did not trust modern medicine; second, it was simply not available. Attitudes are already changing. The curative rites of the yatiris, so appropriate in their campo context, have little meaning on the coast. As men work outside their Aymara setting more and more, they will increasingly return to the campo with a selective set of values derived from the modern world. Modern medicine is obviously more effective, and its introduction into the campo will not be seriously disruptive. Many curanderos are already prescribing antibiotics along with their herbs. A flu epidemic will be treated mostly by druggists in Ilave or Puno, who will prescribe some tablets to one person, and these tablets will be purchased and used over a wide area. Despite laws to the contrary, all drugs can be purchased over the counter without a prescription, and the campesino is rapidly developing a surprisingly apt, if sometimes dangerous, pharmaceutical knowledge for many common complaints.

The health promoter program, begun by Catholic missionaries and in the process of being taken over by the government as I left, is involved in training campesinos in diagnosis and simple curing by modern methods. One or two young men with sufficient literacy are voted by the community to attend classes and to help in the town postas for on-the-job training. Over a period of years, these men can become quite proficient. The program has had its difficulties--promoters were expected to perform altruistically rather than accept payment, many communities voted men not on merit but because they held no other official position--but, by and large, the program was excellently conceived and offers a real hope for significant change. In addition, the government will send nurses periodically to communities that have shown sufficient interest in health to build their own clinics, for which the government supplies standard architectural plans.

Children are more susceptible to fatal dysentery and pneumonia if they or their mothers are malnourished. The campo diet is significantly lacking in proteins, and in vitamins A, C, and B_2. Paradoxically, this problem may be partially alleviated by the diminishment in land per family. Until recently, the Aymara ate only what they could grow themselves, which meant mostly potatoes, oca, barley, and quinoa. Except for broad beans, there were no vegetables, and there was no fruit at all. Meat was eaten only during fiestas or when an aging animal was sacrificed for a rite.

The money economy cannot help but diversify the diet. Oranges from the jungle are already surprisingly popular; they are even sold in the tiny Wednesday morning market in Soqa. Onions, almost never grown by subsistence farmers, were a staple for the family with which I lived. Carrots and peppers are available cheaply in town markets. In addition, workers in Camaná return with large bags of rice which they receive as part of their pay.

Modern medicine and diversification of diet may well reduce the child mortality rate in the future. If that rate were reduced by no more than 50% of the first year's mortality, the population would rise rapidly. The Aymara do have crude means of family planning--herbal abortion and some infanticide--but many women would certainly prefer

148

that more of their children live. There was a sharp
limit on the economic value of children in subsistence agriculture times, because a family had
only a limited amount of land to work, and part of
that land had to be given away when a son or daughter
married. Today, any young man of age to go to the
coast and work is an asset, so there are few limits
on the number of boys that can be profitably raised.

When the population does begin to grow, all of
the changes suggested above will be magnified.
Pressure on the land, already producing to capacity
and still insufficient for family subsistence, will
increase; more men will work outside the community;
larger percentages of family subsistence will depend
on money income; bilingualism and formal education
will become increasingly important; community
systems will have to open up even more than they
are today.

WHERE THE SYSTEM IS HEADING

Can these changes continue indefinitely? That
is, can these processes establish what Francesca
Cancian (1960) refers to as a "moving equilibrium"
in which it is the rate of change that remains
stable, as for example, in the United States? The
answer is an unequivocal "No." Such an equilibrium
requires a theoretically unlimited resource base;
the United States has managed it partially by
systematically exploiting the resources of the rest
of the world. The limits on the altiplano are all
too fixed. Agriculture has already reached its
limits, cattle fattening is very near that point,
and the potential for large-scale governmental
or private investment in the Titicaca Basin is, at

149

the moment, nil. This means that migration, permanent or circular, will remain the major means of
adaptation.

Of these alternatives, permanent migration is
the least adaptive. Massive "invasions" from the
sierra have ringed Lima with hundreds of pueblos
jovenes or barriadas, huge slums with houses constructed of straw matting, populated by literally
millions of people seeking work. Such slums have
grown up around Tacna and other coastal cities as
well, creating intense pressure for full-time work.
The economy cannot expand fast enough to provide
year-round work for all those who need it.

Circular migration is by far the better alternative, as the Aymara themselves clearly recognize.
Under this system, one twelve-month job can provide
work for three or four people instead of one. I
have been told that during planting or harvest, it
is yet possible to be sure of finding a job in the
rice chacras at Camaná or Tambo. So much is this
the case that growers compete with each other for
labor by offering pisco and rice supplements to
wages. The worker who keeps a foot in both the
industrial and agricultural worlds is totally
dependent on neither, so less subject to the
whims of weather or of economic fluctuation. He
retains his land, family, home, kin, community,
and culture, yet he can, happily in many cases,
escape them for a few months out of the year.

Though circular migration can handle three to
four times as many workers as permanent migration,
it, too, has its limits. So far, perhaps half of
the altiplano communities are so lacking in land
and tortora that they need send a high percentage

150

of their men to the coast for several months each year. Unless jungle colonization is expanded significantly--and there is little prospect of this because of the shortage of roads and the cost of building them--the other half will also have to enter the system of circular migration. This will create more pressure for temporary work, and may reduce the number of months a year that it is possible to work. But given a steady rate of industrial and agricultural expansion on the coast, the system should continue to function into the predictable future.

All present trends suggest that the altiplano is moving toward a new economic plateau that will involve agriculture and circular migration in more or less equal measures. There is no trend toward growing for the market or toward collectivization of minifunda lands. People will continue to grow crops for their own families' consumption, and supplement this with money income derived from temporary work on the coast. We may expect the social changes accompanying this transition to level out well before Aymara cultural identity is seriously threatened.

Figure 8.1 illustrates how the collapse of the economic subsystem based on subsistence agriculture set in motion processes which are leading to a new and fundamentally different steady state.

Barring significant government intervention, which appears unlikely at this writing, this process is inevitable and inexorable. The fact that the culture has not broken down under the pressure of these changes suggests that anthropology may have long been underestimating the capacity of peasants

to adapt to new conditions very rapidly. The
Aymara are not merely enduring these changes; many
are enjoying them.

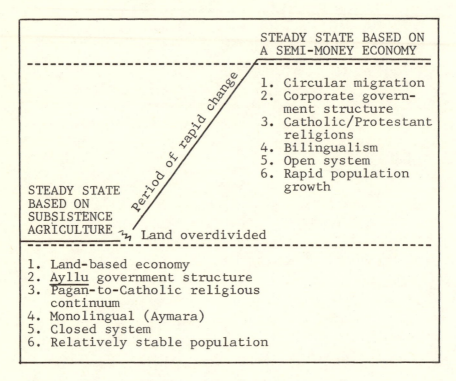

Figure 8.1   Toward a new "steady state"

152

9. Peasants in Transition: Toward a General Model

While many of the "classical" works on peasants emphasize their relation to regional markets or preindustrial cities to which peasants transfer their surplus (e.g., Tax 1976; Foster 1967a: 6-7; Kroeber 1948: 248; Redfield 1960: 2), there has been a growing body of literature which has focused on migration as a primary force in the transition from the subsistence agriculture economy to the money economy. It may be too early, and in any case is not within the scope of this study, to formulate a cross-cultural model of peasant transformation. However, certain general controversies are already manifest, such as the nature of "peasant" and "proletarian," the relation of circular migration to the proletarianization of peasants, the extent to which temporary or seasonal migration is disruptive to family and community organization, and the degree to which factors internal or external to the peasant system are responsible for setting the process in motion. It is hoped that the Aymara case can provide new ethnographic data relevant to these general problems.

PEASANT AND PROLETARIAN

Attempts to precisely define "peasants" have to
a great extent been abandoned as unproductive. While
many definitions retain a continuing value, they may
have a certain static quality, and they may obscure
the more important aspects of particular peasantries.
Some definitions, focusing on relations with regional
markets or on the transfer of surplus to dominant
power holders (Wolf 1966: 3, 11) may be inapplicable
to cases such as the Aymara.

If peasantries are indeed everywhere changing,
perhaps we need less a confining static definition
as a flexible model, with "peasants" viewed not as
a particular type but as a number of possible types
along a continuum. This continuum would include
various degrees of attachment to agriculture and
various degrees of relationship to a wider economic
system. Most peasants would fall somewhere between
the two poles of the family living almost entirely
by subsistence agriculture and the landless proletarian, "engaged in a productive mechanism which
separates him from his family...with an individual
relationship to his employers and productive machine
...but no authority in the production process"
(Miller 1966: 782).

Frucht (1971: 190) assumes a Marxian viewpoint
on this continuum, distinguishing means of production
from relations of production, the latter referring
to such factors as division of labor, social organization, and property and power relations. In
Nevis, a Caribbean island where a type of temporary
migration similar to that of the Aymara is common,
he found a "peasant-like means of production"

154

combined with "proletarian-like relations of production," that is, traditional agriculture on small
plots was combined with sale of labor for wages.
Frucht finds such contrary means and relations
possible only in the context of marginal and perhaps
only capitalist economies.

Such a situation is only contradictory if
viewed from above, from a pre-established theoretical
viewpoint. From the position of the peasant community itself, there is no such contradiction; Aymara
society developed its present mixed economy largely
from its own internal mechanisms, and as logically
and self-consistently as it developed such practices as fattening cattle. Considering the great
number of societies that combine peasant agriculture
with wage labor, we can hardly view such groups as
anomalous, or view peasants and "proletarians" as
contradictory or even contrary types.

If the peasant-proletarian mixture were always
a transitional phase from one extreme to the other,
then perhaps these absolute categories would have
some value after all. We must, therefore, ask to
what extent circular migration is a phase in the
"proletarianization" of peasants.

MIGRATION AND PROLETARIANIZATION

Between 1950 and 1960 an estimated 649,000
rural people, mostly from the sierra, migrated to
urban areas in Peru--13.6% of the entire rural
population (Barraclough and Domike 1970: 68). The
vast majority of these were not Aymara but Quechua,
who form by far the largest Indian-language group
in Peru. Solomon Miller (1966) has studied Quechua
migration in northern Peru and offers a model that

155

may be suggestive for the Aymara, especially as it contradicts my model shown in Figure 8.1.

Prior to mid-century, sugar cane plantations on the coast could not get enough labor. In the 1950's, however, a large Quechua migration to the coast commenced. It should be noted that this time period coincides with my estimates of the time when overpopulation forced the breakdown of the tradition-al subsistence agriculture economy among some Aymara, so similar mechanisms might be involved in northern Peru. In any case, there was soon a labor glut on the coast, which was intensified by the mechanization of the plantations. As the labor market closed up, many temporary or seasonal migrants began to hold on to any jobs they might have or to develop the skills that would procure them permanent jobs. Thus there were three distinct phases in the proletarian-ization of the Quechua studied by Miller: (1) the peasant phase of stabilized agriculture; (2) the transitional phase when workers oscillated between coast and sierra; and (3) the proletarian phase when workers became permanently settled on the coast.

This is hardly a unique case. Arrighi (1973) found a similar proletarianization of peasants in Africa, but related this not to population pressure or mechanization of industry but to wages. The determining factor in this case, according to Arrighi, is the "effort-price" of wage labor. Benefits from migratory work must be sufficient to override the extra effort involved. The reason large-scale proletarianization took so long was not, as earlier theorists held, because of the unfamiliarity of industrial opportunities, but rather because wages were so low they could only support single men.

Workers could not keep families or save for old age on such wages, so were forced to retain tribal ties. When companies found they could get higher productivity from a stabilized labor force and began to pay accordingly, permanent migration became common. Arrighi notes that in the agricultural sector, where stabilization and skilled labor mattered least, wages remained low.

Another case of more or less complete proletarianization is described by Friedl (1974) for the Swiss village of Kippel. After World War II, many natives of the area became "worker-peasants," migrating regularly to wage jobs in urban areas and "willing to give up agriculture as a source of livelihood but not as a way of life" (pg. 82). However, there has been a slow decline in the amount of attention devoted to agriculture, to the point that today nobody in the village is involved solely in agriculture, and most have become workers with very little practical interest in the land.

While examples in which circular migration was indeed a transitional phase in a continuous process of proletarianization might be multiplied, there are certainly other cases where the "worker-peasant" has become an ongoing type that never does become a proletarian (i.e., wage laborer). Rudolfo Stavenhagen (1975: 56-58) describes massive seasonal migrations in both Africa and Latin America. Bracerisimo, the seasonal migration of Mexican peasants to the United States, involves half a million men each year. In regard to Peru, Miller only accounts for the less than 14% of permanent migrants to the coast. If my figures for the altiplano reflect the northern situation, then the majority of workers

remain unaccounted for by the proletarianization
model.

Very often circular migration can be seen,
after the fact, to have been part of a transition
from peasant to proletarian. However, the millions
of people who have been migrating and returning for
many years cannot all be in a transitional phase.
Despite the great urbanization which has taken place
worldwide, few, if any, economies could absorb all
of these migrants as full-time, year-round workers.
Also, most seasonal migration is based on agriculture, which needs large inputs of labor only at
certain times each year and could not support such
a labor force year round. Mechanization of farms
would, of course, reduce such reliance on temporary
migrant labor, but such farms could only absorb a
small percentage of workers. The rest would not be
proletarianized; they would be unemployed.

The proletarianization model is true for some,
including, certainly, many Aymara. It is unaccept-
able insofar as it views circular migration as inevitably a transition phase. The Aymara situation
suggests that in the future, as more and more men
move into the labor market, there may be a labor
glut on the coast with a resulting lowering of wages
and increasing unemployment. But unless long-term
jobs become available, for most temporary migrants
such a situation would only make them more reliant
on what little land is left them in the sierra.
Permanent migration will doubtlessly increase as
population grows, but the majority may remain
worker-peasants for generations to come.

EFFECTS ON HOME COMMUNITY SOCIAL ORGANIZATION

A common view of the modernization of peasants is that this process is disruptive, leading to cultural collapse, to anomie, and possibly even to violent revolt (Smelser 1971: 367-71). In Africa, according to Stavenhagen (1975: 57), mass circular migrations "create a complete disequilibrium between the populations of the cities and the countryside, which aggravates the already acute agrarian crisis, and totally destroys the economic harmony of the African countries and territories directly affected."

However, such negative results must be viewed as potentialities, not as necessities, of the modernizing process. In the Aymara case, large-scale circular migration has not been particularly disruptive, either to the men involved or to their families and communities. This is far from an isolated situation.

Gulliver observes that, while long-term migration of the Ngoni of Tanzania may be difficult for wives and families,

> the individual peasant-family economy is little affected by the ordinary short-term absence of the husband-father, nor do wives and children encounter grave disabilities. In the short view, the family gains from the money and goods brought back by the returning migrant (1955: 42).

Nancie Gonzalez (1961: 1266-68) concluded from her cross-cultural study of the relation between family organization and different types of migratory labor that "seasonal migration per se has little or no determining effect on family organization" and that "family organization is little affected by temporary, non-seasonal migration." Indeed, circular

migration often actually prevented the disruption of
threatened traditional social organization, and
led, not to abrupt change, but to change that was
gradual and non-violent.

THE "INITIAL KICK"

According to Andrew Pearse:

> If our hypothesis is correct, and if today's
> rural change is due to the impact of the modern-
> izing industrial urban society on traditional
> rural communities, then the major factors
> initiating change in rural social systems are
> external to them (1970: 34).

Similarly, as we saw above, Arrighi (1973) relates
the proletarianization of African peasants to wages.
Friedl (1974: 88) saw the rapid rise in emigration
from Kippel as a result of better economic opportunities outside the village.

The Aymara data are in direct contradiction to
any general theory that peasant transformation is
induced exclusively or even largely from without the
peasant system. Once the boundaries of the Aymara
community system are identified, it becomes evident
that the internal dynamics of this system forced
the change. Given exponential population growth on
a limited land base, the ultimate breakdown of the
traditional subsistence agriculture economy could
have been predicted fifty years ago, and without
recourse to considerations of the system's wider
environment. The peasants of this study moved into
the money economy only when they had to, and the
fact that they had to was a result of the internal
dynamics of the Aymara peasant system.

This probably cannot be generalized, for in
the exceptional case when industrialization occurs
within the very midst of a peasant community (e.g.,

Nash 19), inputs from the system's environment will
certainly be the major factor. However, as in the
Aymara case, when industrialization takes place far
from the peasant community, the wage labor option
may only be chosen when internal instabilities make
it necessary.

We can, then, suggest a rough generalization;
the "initial kick" that sets in motion the economic
transformation of a peasant society is likely to
come from the internal processes of the peasant
system itself; but the _form_ which such a transformation will take--whether colonization, development of home industries, or circular migration--
will be largely determined by the options offered
by the system's wider environment.

SUMMARY

Data for the Aymara transition from subsistence
agriculture to the money economy is sufficiently
in line with other studies in which circular migration has been a key element in peasant change that
it would appear that a general model of peasant
transformation may indeed be possible in the future.
Some of the elements of such a model have been suggested above. "Peasants" should be defined very
broadly and along a continuum. Circular migration
is, for some, a transitional stage to becoming
urban-dwelling wage laborers, but for many others
it is a steady state in itself, and the worker-
peasant can be an enduring type. If only circular
migration for short periods is involved, neither the
worker's family nor community need suffer much
disruption. Finally, the initial kick for peasant
transformation may be the result of processes

within the peasant system itself, though the means
by which such a transformation is accomplished will
be determined by the system's wider environment.

Appendixes

A. How the Data Was Collected and Analyzed

Before the questionnaire was written I had spent
three months in the altiplano teaching anthropology
to the missionaries, had spent two months of preliminary investigation, and had lived with a
campesino family in Soqa for four months, so I had
by this time a fairly good idea of the type of
information I wanted and what sort of questions would
be so threatening that they should be left out. At
the time of writing the questionnaire I was not
aware of the extent of the economic transformation
going on around me, so it was largely written to
test economic and attitudinal differences between
Catholics and Adventists. The questionnaire would
be in three parts: a general census, an economic
section, and attitudes. The economic section would
be the most extensive, and most important, though
in order to avoid threatening the people, who were
afraid of the imposition of taxes or collectivization of their land, I would include no questions
about money or land possession.

A test questionnaire was given to about thirty-
five family heads in Soqa and Pampankiri by the
presidents of each community. I found that many of
my economic questions were not specific enough and

that the people refused to respond to such attitudinal questions as "The Maryknoll missionaries are here to deceive the people"--agree or disagree. For the final version, I made the necessary corrections and added a number of attitude questions.

Almost all the attitude questions were based on the questionnaire given by Hickman (1971) in 1962 in six communities around Chinchera. This made possible a certain time-depth study, when my scores and his were compared, though I allowed only two choices (agree, disagree) while Hickman allowed three (agree, partially agree, disagree). The reasons for my decision to diverge from the Hickman questionnaire on this point were, first, to make it easier to give the questionnaire, and, second, I felt that too many of Hickman's respondants were using the "partially agree" answer to avoid really giving an opinion.

Hickman's questionnaire consisted of 176 questions, and the categories I was seeking--traditonalism, insecurity, status of women, orientation to capitalism, value of education, and fatalism--were well represented, so I only had to add a few of my own questions (questions B, 11, and 15). In selecting questions, I had the advantage of Hickman's original scores plus his factor analysis, which showed which questions had been interpreted to have the strongest relation to traditionalism and insecurity.

THE SAMPLES

In the altiplano, it is not always easy to get any sample at all, since many people, and entire communities, simply refuse to take a questionnaire.

THE SAMPLE

	Families in sample	Total Families	Sample as % of total
Soqa (Catholic and Adventist)	165	267	62%
Pampankiri (all Catholic)	128	130	98%
Qollu K'uchu (Catholic and Adventist)	60	100 (est.)	60% (est)

SOQA ONLY

Sector	Families in Adv. sample	Families in Cath. sample	Total sample	Total no. families	Sample as % of total
Chaulluta	21	20	41	42	98%
Huilamaya	11	36	47	53	89%
Huallatani	9	45	54	55	98%
Suopatja	3	14	17	49	35%
Soqapatja	2	4	6	34	18%
Umatunta	0	0	0	34	00%
Totals	46	119	165	267	62%
	(98% of Adventists; 17% of community)	(56% of Catholics; 45% of community)			

166

A statistically random sample was out of the question. Instead, I sought to get as close to 100% as possible for four of Soqa's six sectors. Two of these sectors, Huilamaya and Chaulluta, had the highest percentages of Adventists on the island, while Huallatani and Suopatja, geographically mirror-images of the other two, had much lower Adventist populations. In addition, I sought an all-Catholic community (Pampankiri) and another mixed Adventist-Catholic community (Qollu K'uchu). The latter took literally months of negotiations, so that I was only able to get about a 60% sample, and that included so many people who were new converts to Adventism or of indeterminate religion that I was not able to make the Adventist-Catholic comparisons that I had hoped. Another criterion in seeking sample communities was that they be geographically diverse: one is a mountainous island, one is on a completely flat lakeside area, and one is situated in a series of valleys and pampas far from the lake.

GIVING THE QUESTIONNAIRE

The four community leaders who gave the questionnaire in their own communities were personally trained by me. I had them give the questionnaire to me before they tried it in the field. Then they were to give only a small sample, which I would correct before they would give any more. They were told to translate questions into Aymara only when the respondent did not understand the Spanish version, and then to translate as directly as possible.

It was understood in Soqa that the community would not receive the 10,000 soles promised for their

167

posta roof until I had all the questionnaires in my hands. In addition, the man who gave the questionnaire was paid. In Pampankiri I paid thirty soles per completed questionnaire to the community as a whole, with which benches were purchased for the consejo. In Qollu K'uchu I paid at the same rate, but two-thirds to the community and one-third to the two persons who gave the questionnaire.

From the outset, I was cognizant of the possibility that an interviewer might simply fill out the questionnaires himself, so I let the interviewers know that I would check the data at random in follow-up interviews. In one case, I did receive a set of twenty faked questionnaires, a fact which was immediately obvious: there was no relation to age and sex in the responses and, as a group, they were statistically absurd. My resulting tantrum frightened this interviewer away for three weeks, but the problem did not arise again.

As the questionnaires came in, over a period of three months, they were coded onto special mimeographed sheets, five questionnaires to a page, so that any single item could be very quickly calculated. Final statistics were computed from these coded sheets.

FOLLOW-UP INTERVIEWS

As noted, the economic section of the questionnaire included only questions as to how many months one worked on the coast, how many bulls were sold, how many people sold produce in the market, etc. Follow-up interviews were largely for the purpose of placing money values on these data. I needed to know the wages paid for various jobs, money expenses on the coast, costs of feeding cattle in the various communities, and earnings of band members, among other things. This information was derived from about thirty interviews, given by me in Soqa and Qollu K'uchu and by an assistant in Pampankiri. These money values were then applied to the questionnaire data to give average incomes. Follow-up interviews were also used to clarify questions arising from questionnaire data. What was the criteria for choosing "most important person" in the community and sector? Why did so few people work outside the community in Qollu K'uchu? Why did this community place such a high value on education?

Certain questions (especially #21, on possessions) were re-given to ascertain that the questionnaire had been given and given properly.

THE LAND-CATTLE QUESTIONNAIRE

Near the end of my field work, it became evident that I had gained sufficient trust in Soqa to attempt to determine land and cattle holdings. A brief survey schedule, consisting of merely headings and columns, was given by the sector vigilantes del campo and their auxiliares. I sought a 100% sample (partially to obtain a better census than I had gotten from the questionnaire) and received nearly this from five of Soqa's six sectors. The last of these data I received the night I left Puno to return to the States.

ACCURACY OF THE DATA

The accuracy of the data depends to some extent on how ego-involving or threatening were the questions on the questionnaire.

Economic data are probably quite accurate.
There seemed to be no threat in talking about how
many months one worked on the coast or in what job.
Later, when I personally interviewed a number of
people on money income from various sources, they
seemed quite willing to give any information I needed. I believe that the separation, often by several
months, between interviews on jobs and interviews
on wages reduced any threat these might have had
together.

While total income is probably fairly accurate,
income entering the community is much less so.
There is no way to test this except to simply ask
how much a person can bring back from the coast
after, say, three months. The answers were extremely diverse, so that the averages given must be
taken as simply suggestive.

Education is an ego-related question, and the
averages probably reflect an even inflation of
perhaps a full grade in Soqa and Pampankiri. The
inflation is probably higher in Qollu K'uchu where
education seems more related to status and self-
image. Also, people may have a tendency to count
a few months of irregular class as a full year.

Another threatening question is that dealing
with child mortality. In both Pampankiri and Soqa
a great number of people refused to answer this
question, or responded with, in some cases, a highly
improbable "zero" children dead. To counter this,
in my final computations I did not include "no
responses" or those with four or more living children
who claimed they had no child deaths. Rough as this
may seem, the three widely divergent communities
showed similar rates, and all agreed with Tschopik's

(1951: 3) published rates.

It is difficult to say how accurate are the
land-cattle data, as I was not around long enough to
do follow-up interviews on this. However, this
material, which I received after all economic
statistics had already been computed, conformed surprisingly closely to what I felt the situation had
to be. Also, the close correspondence between different sectors--which were surveyed by different
men and delivered to me at different times--suggests
that these data are more accurate than I might have
expected. This may be partially because vigilantes
del campo and their auxiliares have a good idea of
what everyone in their sector possesses, so it
would have been difficult for a respondent to lie.

B. The Questionnaire

> (a) Community_____
> (b) Sector_____
> (c) No. bldgs. for living__
> (d) No. calamina roofs_____

Put an "X" beside the respondent.

☐ 1. NAME OF MALE HEAD
OF HOUSEHOLD_____Age_____

Education_____

(a) Principal occupation_____

(b) Secondary occupation_____

(c) Official or religious
office_____

(d) Religion ☐Catholic ☐Adventist ☐Other

(e) Were you born in this religion?☐Yes☐No

☐ 2. NAME OF WIFE OR
HOUSEKEEPER_____Age_____

Education_____

3. AGES OF SONS (a) ___ ___ ___   (Put a check
beside those
___ ___ ___ ___ ___ ___ who do not
live in the
AGES OF DAUGHTERS (b) ___ ___ house)

___ ___ ___ ___ ___

4. HOW MANY CHILDREN HAVE DIED? (include all)_____

Ages ___ ___ ___ ___ ___

5. OTHERS WHO LIVE IN THIS HOUSE

Relation _____ Age_____ Education_____
(name not _____ _____ _____
necessary)

_____ _____ _____

6. NAMES OF FATHER AND   Father_____
   MOTHER OF THE MALE
   HEAD OF HOUSEHOLD   Mother_____

7. NAMES OF FATHER AND   Father_____
   MOTHER OF WIFE OR
   HOUSEKEEPER   Mother_____

8. WHO IS THE RICHEST MAN IN YOUR COMMUNITY?

   _____

   In your sector?_____

9. WHO IS THE MOST IMPORTANT MAN IN YOUR COMMUNITY?

   _____

   In your sector?_____

****
THIS SECTION ONLY FOR CATHOLICS

10. FOR WHICH FIESTAS HAVE YOU BEEN ALFERADO DURING
    THE FIVE YEARS JUST PAST?

FIESTA	YEAR	TOTAL COST	COST OF MUSIC	HOW WERE YOU CHOSEN?	COULD YOU REFUSE?

11. DO YOU BELONG TO A DANCE GROUP?   ☐ Yes   ☐ No
    How many pairs are there in your group?_____
    How much does it cost per pair to dance during
    a year? (Detail below)

FIESTA	COST OF MUSIC	COST OF COSTUME

173

THE REST ARE FOR <u>EVERYONE</u>

12. DO YOU WORK OUTSIDE THE COMMUNITY? ☐ Yes ☐ No
    How much time each year?_____
    Where?_____ What type of work?_____
    _____   _____

13. DO YOU PLAY IN A BAND TO EARN MONEY? ☐ Yes ☐ No
    How many times do you play a year?_____

14. DO YOU SELL PART OF YOUR HARVEST IN THE MARKET?
    ☐ Yes ☐ No

15. DO YOU SELL CATTLE? ☐ Yes ☐ No
    Where?_____How many bulls per year_____
    Cows?_____ Others?_____
    Do you raise all the cattle you sell, or buy
    some in order to fatten and resell?
    Raise___ Buy___ How many do you buy a year?___

16. DO YOU HAVE A BUSINESS OF ANY OTHER KIND?
    ☐ Yes ☐ No   What kind?_____
                     Where?_____

17. DO YOU EARN MONEY IN ANY WAY NOT MENTIONED?
    ☐ Yes ☐ No   How?_____
                     Where?_____

18. HAVE YOU VISITED OR WORKED AT ANY TIME IN THE
    FOLLOWING PLACES? (Put a "V" for visit and a
    "T" for work (<u>trabajar</u>))
    (a) Ilave_____ (d) Bolivia_____ (g) Lima_____
    (b) Juliaca_____ (e) Toquepala___ (h) La Selva_
    (c) Arequipa____ (f) Cuzco_____ (i) Tacna_____

19. DO YOU SEND YOUR CHILDREN TO THE ADVENTIST
    SCHOOL?
          ☐ Yes ☐ No   How many children?_____

174

20: HAVE YOU TAKEN A LOAN FROM THE BANCO AGRO-
PECUARIO AT ANY TIME? ☐ Yes ☐ No

How many times in the last five years? _____

For what did you use the loan? _____

21. DO YOU POSSESS THE THINGS THAT FOLLOW?

☐ (a) Bed frame   ☐ (g) Lantern

☐ (b) Primus or other   ☐ (h) Radio
       kerosene stove

☐ (c) Table   ☐ (i) Latrine

☐ (d) Chairs   ☐ (j) Bicycle

☐ (e) Sewing machine   ☐ (k) Motorcycle

☐ (f) Flashlight   ☐ (l) Truck

★★★

INSTRUCTIONS: THE FOLLOWING QUESTIONS ARE NOT OF
FACTS BUT OF YOUR OPINIONS. EACH QUESTION HAS
THREE OR MORE ANSWERS. SELECT THE ONE THAT
IS CLOSEST TO WHAT YOU THINK.

A. WHAT IS THE MOST IMPORTANT OBJECTIVE IN LIFE?

☐ 1. TO EARN A LOT OF MONEY.
☐ 2. TO WELL EDUCATE YOUR CHILDREN.
☐ 3. TO ENJOY LIFE.
☐ 4. TO EARN THE RESPECT OF THE COMMUNITY.

B. IF YOU HAD NOW 10,000 SOLES TO DO WITH AS YOU
LIKE, HOW WOULD YOU SPEND IT?

☐ 1. GIVE A FIESTA.
☐ 2. USE IT ON YOUR FAMILY.
☐ 3. BUY CATTLE TO FATTEN AND SELL.
☐ 4. EDUCATE YOUR CHILDREN.
☐ 5. INVEST IN A BUSINESS, LIKE A SHOP.

C. HOW OFTEN DO YOU GO TO CHURCH?

☐ 1. EACH WEEK.
☐ 2. FROM TIME TO TIME.
☐ 3. ALMOST NEVER OR NEVER.

D. IN YOUR OPINION, THE PRINCIPAL OBJECTIVE OF
RAISING CATTLE IS:

☐ 1. TO DEMONSTRATE TO EVERYONE THE WEALTH OF THE
OWNER.

☐ 2. FOR FOOD AND WOOL.
☐ 3. TO SELL IN ORDER TO EARN MONEY.

E. THE BEST INHERITANCE FOR CHILDREN IS:

☐ 1. EDUCATION.
☐ 2. LAND.
☐ 3. MONEY.

F. IN THESE DAYS IN WHICH THE POPULATION IN THE
    CAMPO IS GROWING WITH SUCH RAPIDITY, THE BEST
    SOLUTION IN ORDER TO HAVE A BETTER LIFE IS:

☐ 1. EMIGRATE TO THE COAST OR TO THE JUNGLE.
☐ 2. JOIN FIELDS IN ORDER TO CULTIVATE THEM IN
     COMMON.
☐ 3. CONTINUE AS NOW.
☐ 4. SELL MORE PRODUCTS--CROPS AND CATTLE--IN
     THE MARKET.
☐ 5. BEGIN A BUSINESS, LIKE A SHOP OR TOURIST
     CRAFTS FACTORY.

****

INSTRUCTIONS: RESPOND TO THE FOLLOWING STATEMENTS
        WITH "AGREE" OR "DISAGREE" ACCORDING TO THAT
        WHICH IS CLOSEST TO WHAT YOU THINK.   THERE ARE
        NO RIGHT OR WRONG ANSWERS.

☐   ☐   1. IT IS BETTER THAT THE PARENTS
Agree Disagree   CHOOSE THE HUSBAND OR WIFE FOR
                      THEIR CHILDREN.

☐   ☐   2. IT IS USELESS TO TRY TO CHANGE
Agree Disagree   ONE'S DESTINY.

☐   ☐   3. THE WOMAN MUST NOT TRY TO BE
Agree Disagree   ANYTHING BUT A MOTHER AND HOUSE-
                      KEEPER.

☐   ☐   4. IN ORDER TO BECOME RICH, IT IS
Agree Disagree   NECESSARY TO CHEAT THE POOR.

☐   ☐   5. WOMEN DESERVE AN EDUCATION EQUAL
Agree Disagree   TO THAT OF MEN.

☐   ☐   6. THE GOAL OF THE PEASANT IS TO
Agree Disagree   PRODUCE A HARVEST IN EXCESS OF
                      PERSONAL NEED TO SELL IN THE
                      NATIONAL MARKET.

☐   ☐   7. MEN ARE ALWAYS MORE INTELLIGENT
Agree Disagree   THAN WOMEN.

176

☐ Agree	☐ Disagree	8. MACHINES MAKE MEN LAZY.
☐ Agree	☐ Disagree	9. COCA AND CARDS TELL THE TRUTH.
☐ Agree	☐ Disagree	10. BY MEANS OF EDUCATION, ONE CAN MAKE OF HIMSELF THAT WHICH HE DESIRES.
☐ Agree	☐ Disagree	11. THERE IS NO CONFLICT BETWEEN THE CATHOLIC RELIGION AND THAT OF OUR ANCESTORS.
☐ Agree	☐ Disagree	12. LIFE IS CHANGING TOO RAPIDLY FOR THE GOOD OF THE PEOPLE.
☐ Agree	☐ Disagree	13. A FAMILY OF ALL DAUGHTERS IS CURSED.
☐ Agree	☐ Disagree	14. SUCCESS IN LIFE DEPENDS MORE ON LUCK THAN ON PERSONAL ABILITY.
☐ Agree	☐ Disagree	15. THE BIRTH OF TWINS SIGNIFIES A PUNISHMENT FROM GOD.
☐ Agree	☐ Disagree	16. IT BOTHERS ME A LOT TO RECEIVE ORDERS.
☐ Agree	☐ Disagree	17. IT IS BETTER NEVER TO PAY MONEY IN ORDER TO GET FOOD.
☐ Agree	☐ Disagree	18. IT IS BETTER TO LIVE IN THE CITY THAN IN THE CAMPO.
☐ Agree	☐ Disagree	19. IN ORDER TO EARN MORE MONEY, IT IS A GOOD IDEA TO TAKE OUT A LOAN FROM THE BANCO AGROPECUARIO.
☐ Agree	☐ Disagree	20. IN ORDER TO HAVE A BETTER LIFE, WE MUST RETURN TO THE TRADITIONAL LIFE OF OUR ANCESTORS.

****

Attitude of respondent: ☐ Good ☐ Normal ☐ Bad

Ability in Spanish: ☐ Good ☐ Normal ☐ Bad

Number of persons present_____

Interviewer_____

C. Statistical Abstract for Three Communities

	SOQA Adv.	SOQA Cat.	Total Soqa	Pampan-kiri	Qollu K'uchu
Sample population	250	527	777	530	289
Males	135	272	407	272	165
Females	115	255	370	258	124
Average family size	5.22	4.43	4.7.	4.14	4.82
Average schooling of adults in years	3.20	2.19	2.47	1.23	3.20
Men	4.47	3.05	3.45	2.00	3.98
Women	2.02	1.41	1.58	0.42	2.43
No. children in Adventist school	32	32	64	0	7
Mortality rates					
To five years	.26	.29	.28	.34	.31
To fifteen years	.30	.30	.30	.36	.32
Political (Soqa only)					
Top six positions	66%	33%	100%		
All non-religious position	37%	63%	100%		
Average number of calamina roofs per family	1.54	1.26	1.34	.83	.63
Took loans from Banco Agropecuario (men respondents only)	.17	.01	.06	.37*	.02
Number that sell produce in the market	.13	.06	.08	.45	.23

*All Pampankiri loans taken out 10-20 years ago.

178

	SOQA Adv.	Cat.	Total Soqa	Pampan- kiri	Qollu K'uchu
Musicians	.15	.04	.07	.00	.19
Average sale of animals per year					
Bulls	1.28	1.22	1.24	2.19	1.30
Cows	.11	.17	.15	.19	.00
Chickens	.02	.02	.02	.10	.00
Pigs	.04	.12	.10	.14	.02
Sheep	.04	.01	.02	.17	.00
Household heads that work outside the community	.70	.75	.74	.60	.36
Types of work: number of workers					
Chacras	.53	.70	.74	.83	.38
Construction	.20	.16	.21	.04	.48
Factories, mines	.20	.07	.10	.03	.00
Types of work: number of months per year per worker					
Chacras	3.6m	4.0	3.9	3.5	1.5
Construction	9.3	5.2	6.5	1.5	2.0
Factories, mines	10.3	12.0	10.8	1.5	0.0
Places of work (number of workers; includes multiple reportings)					
Ilo	.27	.13	.17	.00	.05
Moquegua	.23	.27	.26	.01	.14
Camaná	.37	.75	.65	.81	.00
Tambo	.10	.26	.22	.00	.00
Arequipa	.06	.02	.03	.01	.10
Tacna	.00	.00	.00	.07	.33
Others (mostly in the altiplano)	.06	.03	.04	.09	.35
Travel (men only)					
Ilave	1.00	1.00	1.00	.99	.98
Juliaca	.95	.98	.97	.66	.36
Arequipa	.85	.89	.88	.65	.14
*Bolivia	.10	.00	.03	.01	.00

*From here on, a single asterisk denotes a significant difference between Soqa Adventists and Catholics as determined by the chi square test at .05 significance level.

	SOQA Adv.	SOQA Cat.	Total Soqa	Pampan-kiri	Qollu K'uchu
Toquepala	.02	.03	.03	.03	.03
Cuzco	.07	.03	.04	.02	.03
Lima	.07	.03	.04	.09	.14
The Jungle	.02	.00	.01	.01	.05
Tacna	.17	.05	.08	.23	.22

Possessions

	SOQA Adv.	SOQA Cat.	Total Soqa	Pampan-kiri	Qollu K'uchu
*Bed	.74	.56	.62	.31	.52
Kerosene stove	.98	.92	.95	.83	.72
*Table	.46	.20	.27	.13	.40
*Chairs	.30	.12	.17	.02	.33
Sewing machine	.52	.44	.46	.05	.48
*Flashlight	.15	.03	.07	.02	.05
*Lantern	.20	.03	.06	.10	.48
Radio	.67	.76	.74	.64	.82
*Latrine	.07	.01	.02	.00	.00
Bicycle	.35	.26	.29	.36	.58
Motorcycle	.02	.03	.03	.00	.00

OPINION QUESTIONS (men respondents only)

		SOQA Adv.	SOQA Cat.	Total Soqa	Pampan-kiri	Qollu K'uchu
A	1	.29	.42	.38	.23	.03
	*2	.34	.11	.17	.19	.86
	3	.37	.48	.45	.37	.07
	4	.00	.00	.00	.20	.03
B	1	.04	.01	.01	.04	.02
	2	.39	.77	.67	.34	.27
	*3	.32	.16	.20	.45	.08
	*4	.20	.03	.08	.14	.39
	5	.07	.00	.02	.26	.15
	no response	.02	.04	.03	.00	.00
C	*1	.11	.00	.07	.01	.31
	2	.50	.32	.36	.67	.68
	3	.15	.68	.57	.32	.00
D	1	.00	.01	.01	.14	.02
	2	.68	.81	.77	.23	.95
	*3	.32	.19	.22	.63	.03
E	*1	.20	.02	.06	.04	.92
	2	.80	.96	.92	.43	.07
	3	.00	.02	.01	.53	.02
F	1	.00	.00	.00	.37	.00
	2	.05	.04	.04	.19	.15
	3	.93	.96	.95	.27	.47
	4	.00	.00	.00	.12	.03
	5	.02	.00	.01	.26	.34

	SOQA Adv.	Cat.	Total Soqa	Pampan-kiri	Qollu Ķ'uchu
"AGREE" OR "DISAGREE" OPINION QUESTIONS ("no responses" not included, so many less than 100%)					
1 yes	.05	.00	.01	.88	.02
no	.95	.98	.97	.10	.98
2 yes	.51	.35	.40	.21	.41
no	.44	.61	.56	.77	.46
3 yes	.54	.48	.49	.69	.64
no	.46	.50	.49	.29	.34
4 yes	.07	.01	.02	.01	.02
no	.93	.99	.98	.96	.98
5 yes	.85	.81	.82	.83	.98
no	.15	.19	.18	.15	.00
6 yes	.15	.21	.19	.78	.80
no	.85	.79	.81	.22	.14
7 yes	.88	.76	.79	.61	.59
no	.12	.19	.17	.38	.37
*8 yes	.20	.05	.09	.36	.97
no	.80	.95	.91	.58	.03
*9 yes	.02	.13	.10	.46	.22
no	.98	.80	.84	.53	.78
*10 yes	.71	.44	.51	.82	.98
no	.27	.55	.47	.11	.00
*11 yes	.61	.27	.36	.10	.20
no	.34	.66	.58	.86	.78
*12 yes	.73	.47	.54	.58	.92
no	.27	.48	.43	.40	.05
*13 yes	.15	.03	.06	.24	.07
no	.83	.97	.94	.76	.92
*14 yes	.34	.12	.18	.89	.97
no	.63	.85	.80	.05	.02
*15 yes	.02	.16	.12	.49	.93
no	.98	.82	.86	.50	.05
*16 yes	.25	.45	.40	.30	.34
no	.75	.54	.59	.70	.54
17 yes	.04	.08	.08	.07	.02
no	.96	.84	.92	.92	.97

		SOQA Adv.	SOQA Cat.	Total Soqa	Pampan-kiri	Qollu K'uchu
18	yes	.39	.39	.39	.52	.34
	no	.61	.59	.60	.46	.64
*19	yes	.29	.04	.09	.69	.00
	no	.68	.95	.89	.30	.97
20	yes	.04	.02	.02	.18	.00
	no	.96	.97	.97	.80	.97

D. Income in Three Communities

	SOQA				
	Adventist	Catholic	Total Soqa	Pampankiri	Qollu K'uchu
WORK OUTSIDE COMMUNITY					
Chacras					
No. persons	16	72	88	57	8
Pay per mo. (soles*)	4,160	4,160	4,160	4,160	4,160
No. months	57	291	358	212	21
TOTAL soles	237,120	1,210,560	1,447,680	881,920	87,360
Construction, minining, factories					
No. persons	12	25	37	6	10
Pay per mo. (soles)	5,200	5,200	5,200	5,200	5,200
Total months	111	129	240	19	20
TOTAL soles	577,200	670,800	1,248,000	98,800	104,000
Other work out					
No. persons	3	1	4	1	3
Pay per mo. (soles)	3,000	7,000	31m @ 3,000	7,000	6,000
Total months	31	12	12m @ 7,000	12	36

*1975 rate of 43.8 soles to the U.S. dollar.

| | SOQA | | | | |
	Adventist	Catholic	Total Soqa	Pampankiri	Qollu K'uchu
TOTAL <u>soles</u>	93,000	84,000	177,000	84,000	214,000
TOTAL INCOME FROM WORK OUTSIDE (in soles)	907,320	1,965,360	2,872,680	1,064,720	407,360
OTHER SOURCES OF INCOME					
Buy/sell bulls					
Base profit (<u>soles</u>)	6,250	6,250	6,250	6,250	6,250
Cost of feed	2,000	2,000	2,000	500	4,000
Profit	4,250	4,250	4,250	5,750	2,250
No. sold per year	59	146	205	280	78
TOTAL profit (<u>soles</u>)	250,750	620,500	871,250	1,610,000	175,500
Sale of cows					
Profit	1,000	1,000	1,000	1,000	1,000
No. sold	5	20	25	24	0
TOTAL profit (<u>soles</u>)	5,000	20,000	25,000	24,000	0
Musicians					
No. persons	6	5	11	0	11
Earnings each per year	18,450	18,450	18,450	0	2,488
TOTAL earnings	110,700	92,250	202,950	0	27,368

184

| | SOQA | | Total Soqa | Pampankiri | Qollu K'uchu |
	Adventist	Catholic			
Market sales					
No. persons	6	7	13	58	14
Sales per year each in soles	937	937	937	937	937
TOTAL earnings	5,622	6,559	12,181	54,346	13,118
TOTAL INCOME OF SAMPLE					
"Work out" + "Other sources" (in soles)	1,279,392	2,704,699	3,984,061	2,753,066	623,346
SAMPLE POPULATION					
No. families	46	119	165	128	60
Average children per family	5.45	4.44	4.72	4.14	4.80
Total population	251	528	779	530	288
PER CAPITA INCOME					
In soles	5,097	5,122	5,114	5,194	2,164
In U.S. dollars (1965)	116	117	117	119	49
PER FAMILY INCOME					
In soles	27,813	22,728	24,146	21,508	10,389
In U.S. dollars	635	519	551	491	237

| | SOQA | | | | |
	Adventist	Catholic	Total Soqa	Pampankiri	Qollu K'uchu
MONEY ENTERING THE COMMUNITY PER FAMILY PER YEAR (1975 U.S. $)*	406	279	314	342	162

*These are estimates of averages brought back from the coast added to average family income for cattle fattening, playing in bands, and market sales.

E. Land and Animal Possession, Soqa

	Cultivated land in hectares	Cattle	Sheep	Pigs	Chickens
Mean	.84	1.33	2.92	.40	.74
Range	.10-4	0-5	0-10	0-7	0-4

*Sample: 189 families.

F. Population Distribution, Soqa

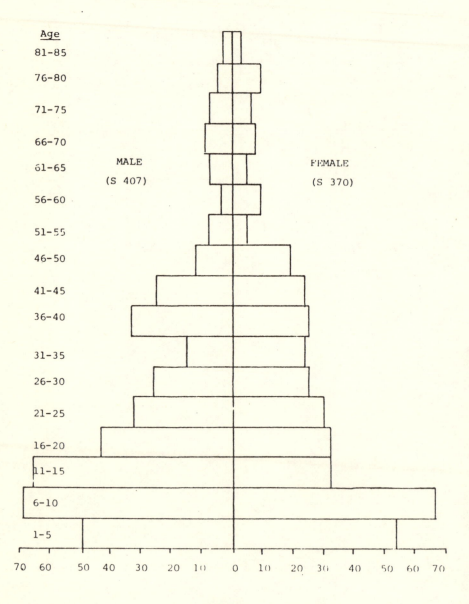

Bibliography

Albo', Javiar
1974 Esposos, suegros y padrinos entre Los
Aymaras. La Paz, Bolivia: Centro de Investi-
gación y Promoción del Campesinado.

Arriaga, Pablo Joseph de
1968 The Extirpation of Idolatry in Peru. Lex-
ington: University of Kentucky Press.

Arrighi, Giovanni
1973 Labor Supplies in Historical Perspective.
In Essays on Political Economy in Africa, by
Giovanni Arrighi and John S. Saul. New York:
Monthly Review Press.

Ashby, W. Ross
1968 Principles of Self-Organizing Systems. In
Modern Systems Research for the Behavioral
Scientist. Walter Buckley, ed. Chicago:
Aldine.

Barraclough, Solon L., and Arthur L. Domike
1970 Agrarian Structure in Seven Latin American
Countries. In Agrarian Problems and Peasant
Movements in Latin America. Rudolfo Stavenhagen, ed. Garden City, N.Y.: Anchor Books.

Bastien, Joseph W.
1974 Qollahuaya Mountain: Symbolism of the Great
Diviners of the Andes. Privately printed.

Belshaw, Cyril S.
1965 Traditional Exchange and Modern Markets.
Englewood Cliffs, N.J.: Prentice-Hall.

Bertalanffy, Ludwig von
1968 General Systems Theory: A Critical Review.
In Modern Systems Research for the Behavioral
Scientist. Walter Buckley, ed. Chicago: Aldine.

Bhagwati, Jagdish
1966 The Economics of Underdeveloped Countries.
New York: World University Library.

Bolton, Ralph
1973 Aggression and Hypoglycemia among the Qolla:
A Study in Psychobiological Anthropology.
Ethnology 12: 227-257.

Buckley, Walter
1967 Sociology and Modern Systems Theory.
Englewood Cliffs, N.J.: Prentice-Hall.

Buechler, Hans C., and Judith-Maria Buechler
1971 The Bolivian Aymara. New York: Holt, Rinehart and Winston.

Cancian, Francesca
1960 Functional Analysis of Change. American
Sociological Review 25:818-827.

Carmona Cruz, Aurielio, et al.
1967 La comunidad de Soqa. Puno, Peru: Instituto
Indigenista Peruana.

Carter, W. E.
1965a Aymara Communities and the Bolivian
Agrarian Reform. Gainesville, Fla.: Social
Science Monographs No. 24.

1965b Innovation and Marginality: Two South
American Case Studies. America Indigina 25:
383-398.

1968 Secular Reinforcement in Aymara Death
Ritual. American Anthropologist 70:238-263.

1972 Trial Marriage in the Andes? Paper read
at the Symposium on Andean Kinship and
Marriage, American Anthropological Association
Meeting, Toronto, 1972. Manuscript in Library
of Instituto de Estudios Aymaras, Chucuito,
Peru.

CIED
1973 Arzuñañi: Una experienca de explotación de
campesinos Aymaras en la comercialización de
ganado. Lima: Centro de Informacion, Estudios
y Documentación.

CISEPA
1967 Rural Puno Before Take-Off. Lima: Centro
de Investigaciones Sociales, Economicas,
Politicas y Antropológicas.

Dalton, George
1971 Economic Anthropology and Development. New

190

York: Basic Books.

Davies, Thomas M., Jr.
1970   Indian Integration in Peru: A Half-Century
of Experience, 1900-1948. Lincoln: University
of Nebraska Press.

Devereaux, George
1961   Two Types of Modal Personality Theory. In
Studying Personality Cross-Culturally. Bert
Kaplan, ed. Evanston: Row, Peterson.

Dew, Edward
1969   Politics in the Altiplano: The Dynamics of
Change in Rural Peru. Austin: University of
Texas Press.

Diaz, May N.
1967   Introduction: Economic Relations in Peasant
Society. In Peasant Society: A Reader. Jack
M. Potter, et al., eds. Boston: Little, Brown.

Dobyns, Henry E., and Paul L. Doughty
1976   Peru: A Cultural History. New York: Oxford
University Press.

Donahue, John M.
1972   Circular Migration in Southern Peru: An
Anthropological Perspective. Manuscript in
the Library of the Instituto de Estudios
Aymaras, Chucuito, Peru.

Douglass, John M.
1970   Peasant Emigrants: Reactors or Actors? In
Migration and Anthropology. Robert F. Spencer,
ed. Proceedings of the 1970 Annual Spring
Meeting of the American Ethnological Society.

Easton, David
1965   A Systems Analysis of Political Life. New
York: John Wiley and Sons.

Epstein, Scarlett
1971   Economic Development and Social Change in
South India. In Economic Development and
Social Change. George Dalton, ed. Garden
City: Natural History Press.

Escobar, Gabriel M.,
1967   Organización social and cultural del sur
del Peru. Mexico City: Instituto Indigenista
Interamericano.

Fallers, L.A.
1971   Are African Cultivators to be Called
"Peasants"? In Economic Development and Social

Change. George Dalton, ed. Garden City:
Natural History Press.

Fisk, E. K., and R. T. Shand
    1965 The Early Stages of Development in a Primi-
        tive Economy: The Evolution from Subsistence
        to Trade Specialization. In Subsistence
        Agriculture and Economic Development. Clifton
        R. Wharton, Jr., ed. Chicago: Aldine.

Foster, George M.
    1967a Introduction: What is a Peasant? In Peasant
        Society: A Reader. Jack M. Potter, et al., eds.
        Boston: Little-Brown.

    1967b Tzintzuntzan: Mexican Peasants in a Chang-
        ing World. Boston: Little-Brown.

Friedl, John
    1974 Kippel: A Changing Village in the Alps. New
        York: Holt, Rinehart and Winston.

Frucht, Richard
    1971 A Caribbean Social Type: Neither "Peasant"
        nor "Proletarian." In Peoples and Cultures of
        the Caribbean. Michael M. Horowitz, ed.
        Garden City, N.Y.: Natural History Press.

Gamst, Frederick
    1974 Peasants in Complex Society. New York:
        Holt, Rinehart and Winston.

Gill, Richard T.
    1964 Economic Development: Past and Present.
        Englewood Cliffs: Prentice-Hall.

Gonzalez, Nancie L. Solien
    1961 Family Organization in Five Types of Migra-
        tory Wage Labor. American Anthropologist 63:
        1264-80.

Gulliver, P. H.
    1955 Labour Migration in a Rural Economy. Lon-
        don: East African Studies No. 6.

Hickman, John Marshall
    1963 The Aymara of Chinchera, Peru: Persistance
        and Change in a Bicultural Context. Unpub-
        lished doctoral dissertation, University
        Microfilms #64-3641.

    1971 Los Aymaras de Chinchera, Peru. Mexico
        City: Instituto Indigina Interamericano.

IIP (Instituto Indigenista Peruana)
    1968 Estudios referentes a cuatro aspectos de
        la IIP - E.A.C. Lima.

Keesing, Roger M.
1976 Cultural Anthropology: A Contemporary Perspective. New York: Holt, Rinehart and Winston.

Kessler, J. B. A., Jr.
1967 A Study of the Older Protestant Missions in
Peru and Chile. Goes, Netherlands: Oosterbaan
and le Cointre.

Kroeber, A. L.
1948 Anthropology. New York: Harcourt, Brace.

LaBarre, Weston
1948 The Aymara Indians of the Lake Titicaca
Plateau, Bolivia. Memoirs of the American
Anthropological Association No. 68.

1966 The Aymara: History and World View. In
The Anthropologist Looks at Myth. J. Green-
way, ed. Austin: University of Texas Press.

Lanning, Edward P.
1967 Peru Before the Incas. Englewood Cliffs,
N.J.: Prentice-Hall.

Mason, J. Alden
1957 The Ancient Civilizations of Peru. Middle-
sex, England: Penguin.

Matos Mar, Jose
1974 Presentación. In Reciprocidad e intercambio
en los Andes peruanos. Lima: Instituto de
Estudios Peruanos.

Means, Philip A.
1931 Ancient Civilizations of the Andes. New
York: Gordian.

Miller, Solomon
1966 Proletarianization of the Indian Peasants
in Northern Peru. Transactions of the New York
Acadamy of Sciences 28:782-89.

Nash, Manning
1966 Primitive and Peasant Economic Systems. San
Francisco: Chandler.

1967 Machine Age Maya. Chicago: University of
Chicago Press.

Ochoa, Victor
1974a Apuntes para una cosmovisión Aymara.
Chucuito, Peru: Instituto de Estudios Aymaras,
Boletin Ocasional, No. 8.

1974b La creencia Aymara del "qharisiri" or
"liq'ichiri." Chucuito, Peru: Instituto de

Estudios Aymaras, Boletin Ocasional, No. 6.

ONEC (Oficina Nacional de Estatistica y Census)
    1972 Poblacion del censo del 4 de Junio. Lima,
    Peru.

Osborne, Harold
    1952 Indians of the Andes: Aymaras and Quechuas.
    London: Routledge and Kegan Paul.

Pearse, Andrew
    1970 Agrarian Change Trends in Latin America.
    In Agrarian Problems and Peasant Movements in
    Latin America. Rudolfo Stavenhagen, ed.
    Garden City, N.Y.: Anchor Books.

Pike, Frederick B.
    1957 The Modern History of Peru. London:
    Weidenfeld and Nicolson.

Potter, Jack M.
    1967 From Peasants to Rural Proletarians: Social
    and Economic Change in Rural Communist China.
    In Peasant Society: A Reader. Jack Potter,
    et al., eds. Boston: Little-Brown.

Quijano Obregon, Anibal
    1968 Tendencies in Peruvian Development and in
    the Class Structure. In Latin America: Reform
    or Revolution? James Petras and Maurice
    Zeitlin, eds. New York: Fawcett.

Rapaport, Anatol
    1968 The Promise and Pitfalls of Information
    Theory. In Modern Systems Theory for the
    Behavioral Scientist. Walter Buckley, ed.
    Chicago: Aldine.

Redfield, Robert
    1960 Peasant Society and Culture. Chicago:
    University of Chicago Press.

Roseberry, William
    1976 Rent, Differentiation, and the Development
    of Capitalism among Peasants. American
    Anthropologist 78:45-58.

Schaedel, Richard P.
    1967 La demografia y los recursos humanos del
    sur del Peru. Mexico City: Instituto Indegi-
    nista Interamericano.

Smelser, Neil J.
    1971 Mechanisms of Change and Adjustments to
    Change. In Economic Development and Social
    Change. George Dalton, ed. Garden City:

                Natural History Press.

Stahl, F. A.
    1920 En el pais de los Incas.   Puno, Peru:
    privately printed.

Stavenhagen, Rudolfo
    1975 Social Classes in Agrarian Societies.
    Garden City, N.Y.: Anchor Books.

Steward, Julian, and Luis C. Faron
    1959 Native Peoples of South America. New York:
    McGraw-Hill.

Tawney, R. H.
    1926 Religion and the Rise of Capitalism. London:
    John Murray.

Tax, Sol
    1976 Penny Capitalism: A Guatamalan Indian
    Economy. New York: Octogon.

Trotter, Robert J.
    1973 Aggression: A Way of Life for the Qolla.
    Science News 103:76-77.

Tschopik, Harry, Jr.
    1946 The Aymara. In Handbook of South American
    Indians, Vol. 2. J. Steward, ed. Bureau of
    American Ethnology Bulletin #143. Washington,
    D.C.: Government Printing Office.

    1951 The Aymara of Chucuito, Peru: Volume I,
    Magic. New York: Anthropological Papers of
    the American Museum of Natural History 44(3).

Weber, Max
    1956 The Protestant Ethic and the Spirit of
    Capitalism. New York: Charles Scribners and
    Sons.

Wolf, Eric
    1966 Peasants. Englewood Cliffs, N.J.: Prentice-
    Hall.